THE RENEWAL OF
CIVILIZATION

THE RENEWAL
OF CIVILIZATION

by
DAVID HOFMAN

'*Soon will the present day order be
rolled up, and a new one spread
out in its stead.*'
BAHÁ'U'LLÁH.

GEORGE RONALD
OXFORD

The cover photograph was kindly supplied by the
Audio-Visual Department of the Bahá'í World Centre.

Printed in U.S.A.

CONTENTS

INTRODUCTION

THIS book contains a story and a message. Its story is one of heroism, of men and women lifted by an all-compelling power to the plane of nobility and martyrdom. Its message is one of hope and assurance.

The progressive disintegration, in this century, of all that was considered stable in the old order of the world, has evoked doubts and fears in every heart. We are apprehensive of the future and question the purpose of life, the value of striving, the good of civilization.

Such questions touch the very foundation of our existence. They go deeper than war, birth or death, which are only transitory moments in the whole of our existence. They lead us to the mystery which has attracted and baffled the human mind as far back as history is recorded. They also, once answered, impel us to action in the very practical way of remaking our society according to the answer which we find. If your answer, for instance, is that the glorification of the state is the aim and end of life, you will try to remould the world on some totalitarian conception. If you say, as the mystics do, that the aim of life is to rejoin the Essence from which you came, you will spend your life in meditation and let the world go hang. If you say there is no purpose in life, as some do, or if you haven't thought much about it, as many haven't, you will find your life becoming more and more uncomfortable, your world disrupting and finally broken, and yourself bewildered and unhappy.

All this, of course, brings us to religion, a highly contentious subject and one which arouses every kind of emotion from passionate disgust to unbearable sanctimoniousness. Let me assure you that although this book is about religion, it holds no brief for creed, ritual, sectarianism or any of the man-made doctrines which have stifled the true spirit of religion.

It is concerned with the spirit of man, and shows how it, like all other living things, grows according to its nature, from season to season, through the influence of the returning sun.

The sun of the human spirit is the Word of God, revealed in every age by the Founders of the great religions. Moses, Jesus, Muḥammad, Krishna, Buddha, were the Mediators through which this sun shone in past ages. Owing to them, great civilizations arose.

Today is another spring time, when in fulfilment of the ancient promises, the spiritual sun has again risen to guide mankind in his hour of darkness, to shed the light of truth upon the difficult problems of the age, and to evoke in human hearts that faith and radiant love which are the first requirements for reconstruction.

The Word of God is revealed today by Bahá'u'lláh (a Persian name meaning Glory of God).

The world religion which he founded is called the Bahá'í Faith, and its purpose is none other than the creation of a world civilization. It offers to mankind a rebirth of spiritual life, together with laws and principles adequate to embody that new spirit in a universal, all-embracing World Order. Its message, and some of its history form the subject of this essay.

CHAPTER I

THE NEW REVELATION

The Seed

The nineteenth century was remarkable in every way. When, in 1815, the Napoleonic age had apparently come to an end, and the rigid Metternich system had subdued the liberalism of Europe, it seemed as though darkness had again enveloped the human spirit.

But there were forces at work within mankind which no tyranny could suppress, and the nations of Europe, one by one, threw off the yoke which had been imposed on them at Vienna. Democracy—and nationalism—triumphed.

Europe was not the only part of the world to feel these new forces. America, pushing its frontier ever westward, was heading towards the great upheaval which settled the two questions of political unity and racial equality, the latter in principle if not in fact. Imperialism was opening up the whole of Africa. Japan was beginning to adopt western methods and to emerge as a great power. Even in Russia and China the old order was being questioned until they too were caught in the whirlpool of change.

These were the visible signs of two great revolutions taking place together. In the west, the industrial revolution was changing ways of life, human relationships and social conditions. In the east, a revolution of a different kind was coming to birth, a spiritual revolution. Both were destined to spread around the world, and by their interpenetration of each other to open the doors of a new era to all mankind.

The Middle East was, at the turn of the century, in a state of decay. The brilliant civilization of Islám, her social order, her arts and sciences, had vanished. Ignorance, dirt and slothfulness, reinforced by fanaticism, were the order of the day. And Persia (now called Írán) had reached the extreme depth of this condition. Her people groaned under the oppression of church and state, whose rapacious cruelty extorted from them everything but the bare means of existence. Corruption, bribery and greed were everywhere apparent and the whole country was steeped in apathy and superstition. Religious prejudice was so fanatical that a Muslim whose clothes were touched by those of a Christian or Jew, considered himself defiled. The priesthood ensured their domination by keeping the people in ignorance and fear. The court indulged in lavish display and the ministers of state occupied themselves with frivolities, while the population diminished and the life of the people became a wearisome burden.

It was in this dark and backward country that the spiritual revolution was born.

At that time there was widespread expectation throughout the Christian world of the second com-

ing of Christ, an attitude encouraged by the
churches.* Islám, divided like Christianity into two
main sections, Sunní and S̲h̲í‘ih, looked for two
messengers, and it is perhaps new to many Christians
that one half expected Jesus Christ.

Through the insight and devotion of two learned
men, S̲h̲ayk̲h̲ Aḥmad and Siyyid Káẓim, a small band
of people had been prepared to seek out and recognize the Promised One, when he should declare
himself.

They believed that his advent was imminent and on
the death of Káẓim, one of them, Mullá Ḥusayn, set
out to seek him. He records that he felt drawn to the
city of S̲h̲íráz, 'as if by a magnet', and that one
evening, as he approached the gate of the city, he
was greeted by a strange youth of radiant coun-
tenance, who wore a green turban and who greeted
him as a lifelong friend.

Mullá Ḥusayn records this incident, and what followed:[1]

'The youth who met me outside the gate of
S̲h̲íráz overwhelmed me with expressions of affection and loving kindness. He extended to me a
warm invitation to visit his home, and there refresh
myself after the fatigues of the journey. I prayed to
be excused, pleading that my two companions had
already arranged for my stay in that city, and were
now awaiting my return.

' "Commit them to the care of God," was his
reply; "He will surely protect and watch over them."

* See Townshend, *The Promise of All Ages*, chap. 1.

'Having spoken these words, he bade me follow him. I was profoundly impressed by the gentle yet compelling manner in which that strange youth spoke to me. As I followed him, his gait, the charm of his voice, the dignity of his bearing, served to enhance my first impressions of this unexpected meeting.

'As I entered the house and followed my host to his chamber, a feeling of unutterable joy invaded my being. Immediately we were seated, he ordered a ewer of water to be brought, and bade me wash away from my hands and feet the stains of travel. I pleaded permission to retire from his presence and perform my ablutions in an adjoining room. He refused to grant my request, and proceeded to pour the water over my hands. He then gave me to drink of a refreshing beverage, after which he asked for the samovar and himself prepared the tea which he offered me.

'Overwhelmed by his acts of extreme kindness, I arose to depart. "The time for evening prayer is approaching," I ventured to observe. "I have promised my friends to join them at that hour."

'With extreme courtesy and calm he replied: "You must surely have made the hour of your return conditional upon the will and pleasure of God. It seems that His will has decreed otherwise. You need have no fear of having broken your pledge."

'His dignity and self-assurance silenced me. I renewed my ablutions and prepared for prayer. He too, stood beside me and prayed. Whilst praying, I unburdened my soul, which was much oppressed, both by the mystery of this interview and the strain and stress of my search. I breathed this prayer:

' "I have striven with all my soul, O my God, and until now have failed to find Thy promised messenger. I testify that Thy word faileth not, and that Thy promise is sure."

'That night, that memorable night, was the eve of the twenty-third of May, 1844.

'It was about an hour after sunset when my youthful host began to converse with me. "Whom, after Siyyid Kázim," he asked me, "do you regard as his successor and your leader?"

' "At the hour of his death," I replied, "our departed teacher insistently exhorted us to forsake our homes, to scatter far and wide in quest of the promised beloved. I have, accordingly, journeyed to Persia, have arisen to accomplish his will, and am still engaged in my quest."

' "Has your teacher," he further inquired, "given you any detailed indications as to the distinguishing features of the promised one?"

' "Yes," I replied, "he is of a pure lineage, is of illustrious descent, and of the seed of Fátimih. As to his age, he is more than twenty and less than thirty. He is endowed with innate knowledge. He is of medium height, abstains from smoking, and is free from bodily deficiency."

'He paused for a while and then with vibrant voice declared: "Behold, all these signs are manifest in me!" '

Mullá Ḥusayn was overwhelmed by this declaration. Throughout that night, he sat at the feet of his master, listening to his proofs, spellbound by the power and charm of his utterance. Before departing, in the early morning, his host addressed to him these words:

'O thou who art the first to believe in Me! Verily I say, I am the Báb, the Gate of God, and thou art the Bábu'l-Báb, the gate of that Gate. Eighteen souls must, in the beginning, spontaneously and of their own accord, accept Me and recognize the truth of My Revelation.'[2]

Within a few days of the Báb's declaration, seventeen people had, by their own spontaneous efforts, found him and recognized his station. These, with Ṭáhirih, the heroine poetess who accepted him without meeting him, were called the Letters of the Living. They were the first disciples and were given the task of penetrating the spiritual darkness of their degenerate country.

The Báb's message was this. A new period in human history had begun, a period which would see the realization of the brotherhood of man, in a new and worldwide order. This great day would be established through the influence of a great Prophet, whom the Báb referred to as 'He Whom God shall manifest'. It was his own mission, the Báb declared, to herald the coming of 'He Whom God shall manifest', and he promised that his appearance was very near. He instructed the Letters of the Living to spread this message throughout the country and to prepare the people for the great event. He told them that they would be persecuted and martyred, and he bade farewell to them with these words:

'O My beloved friends! You are the bearers of the name of God in this Day. . . . It behoves each one of you to manifest the attributes of God, and to exemplify by your deeds and words the signs of His righteousness, His power and glory. The very members of your body must bear witness to the loftiness of your purpose, the integrity of your life, the reality of your faith, and the exalted character of your devotion. . . . Ponder the words of Jesus addressed to His disciples, as He sent them forth to propagate the Cause of God. In words such as these, He bade them arise and fulfil their mission: "Ye are even as the fire which in the darkness of the night has been kindled upon the mountain-top. Let your light shine before the eyes of men. Such must be the purity of your character and the degree of your renunciation, that the people of the earth may through you . . . be drawn closer to the heavenly Father Who is the Source of purity and grace . . . You are the salt of the earth, but if the salt have lost its savour, wherewith shall it be salted?" . . . O My Letters! . . . you are the witnesses of the Dawn of the promised Day of God. . . . Purge your hearts of worldly desires, and let angelic virtues be your adorning. . . . The days when idle worship was deemed sufficient are ended. The time is come when naught but the purest motive, supported by deeds of stainless purity, can ascend to the throne of the Most High and be acceptable unto

Him. . . . I am preparing you for the advent of a mighty Day. Exert your utmost endeavour that, in the world to come, I, who am now instructing you, may, before the mercy-seat of God, rejoice in your deeds and glory in your achievements. The secret of the Day that is to come is now concealed. It can neither be divulged nor estimated. The newly born babe of that Day excels the wisest and most venerable men of this time, and the lowliest and most unlearned of that period shall surpass in understanding the most erudite and accomplished divines of this age. Scatter throughout the length and breadth of this land, and, with steadfast feet and sanctified hearts, prepare the way for His coming. Heed not your weaknesses and frailty; fix your gaze upon the invincible power of the Lord, your God, the Almighty. Has He not, in past days, caused Abraham, in spite of His seeming helplessness, to triumph over the forces of Nimrod? Has He not enabled Moses, whose staff was His only companion, to vanquish Pharaoh and his hosts? Has He not established the ascendancy of Jesus, poor and lowly as He was in the eyes of men, over the combined forces of the Jewish people? Has He not subjected the barbarous and militant tribes of Arabia to the holy and transforming discipline of Muḥammad, His Prophet? Arise in His name, put your trust wholly in Him, and be assured of ultimate victory.' [3]

The Letters fulfilled their mission and died as martyrs to their faith. Within the short span of six years Írán was electrified by the new message and it

became the principle issue of life, Bábí or not Bábí.
The priesthood, seeing their position threatened by
the enlightenment of the people, arose with fierce
hatred to exterminate the Báb and his followers.
The Bábís, shut off from their leader by his imprisonment, and not fully understanding the spirit
of the new revelation, defended themselves by arms.
The whole power of the state was brought to their
destruction.

A period of incredible chaos followed. The Báb
became the centre of a storm fiercer even than that
which raged around the founder of Christianity. Of
the bitter persecution inflicted on his followers, of
the stirring deeds of valour which he inspired, of his
own irresistible charm and radiance, many historians
have written. To quote but one, Lord Curzon:
'Tales of magnificent heroism illumine the blood-
stained pages of Babi history . . . and the fires of
Smithfield did not kindle a nobler courage than has
met and defied the more refined torture-mongers of
Teheran.' [4]

In the course of a few years twenty thousand men,
women and children were martyred in circumstances
of horrible cruelty. The Báb himself, after but six
years of ministry, during which time he was subjected to imprisonment and other forms of persecution, was sentenced to death and executed by a firing
squad in Tabríz. The authorities hoped that the loss
of its leader would mean the end of the heresy, but
no opposition could dim the radiance of those brilliant hearts. The land was terror-ridden; the Báb

was martyred; but still the Bábís came in their thousands to water with their life-blood the seed of the Day which it was their privilege to announce.

Who were these contemptible heretics, daring to accept a new Prophet after Muḥammad and to challenge the power of the priests? Let them be exterminated! So ruthless and thorough was the persecution that it seemed as though it might accomplish its purpose. Finally there remained but one person of influence, whose qualities of leadership and moral authority could have sustained the bruised and scattered Bábís. His name was Ḥusayn-'Alí, later Bahá'u'lláh. Him, the forces of opposition imprisoned, bastinadoed, and finally banished, with his family and a few friends to Baghdád, beyond the confines of Persia.

The followers of the Báb were left broken and exhausted, deprived of all their resources and of the counsel of their leaders, in danger of their lives. Had their sacrifices been in vain? Was this gleam in the Persian sky but a flashing meteor, or did it betoken the true sunrise for mankind? Only the future could tell.

The Tree

Mírzá Ḥusayn-'Alí was born in Ṭihrán on November 12th, 1817. His father was a nobleman of great wealth, holding an important ministerial appointment at the court of the Sháh. This post was offered to Mírzá Ḥusayn-'Alí at his father's death, but he refused it. His interests lay elsewhere.

'This youthful scion of a house of nobility had an overwhelming passion for justice. He deserted the court to tend the oppressed and the aggrieved. Not once did He hesitate to champion the cause of the poor and the fallen who turned to Him for succour and help. None who deserved was refused. Thus passed the days of His Youth, until a day came when an emissary set out with a letter to seek Him, and the very qualities that made Him a haven and refuge, and raised Him in the esteem of His fellowmen, convinced that emissary that the Son of the late minister from Núr was indeed the Exalted Person intended to receive the letter of the Báb.' [5]

Mullá Ḥusayn was the bearer of this message, and he was able to tell his Master, the Báb, that its truth had been instantly accepted. 'Thus at the age of twenty-seven, the Son of the minister, Who had withdrawn from the life of the court, the brilliant nobleman Whose sense of justice was a byword amongst all who knew Him, Whose knowledge, eloquence and lovable nature were exemplary, put Himself on the side of a religious renaissance that was bound to excite the hatred of the ruling classes of the realm.' [6]

The Báb and his noble ally never met, but the Báb knew that Mírzá Ḥusayn-'Alí would one day fulfil his own promise, and would appear as 'He Whom God shall manifest', the source of unity and guidance to a world soon to be caught in the throes of the most tremendous upheaval of its history. It was the Báb who designated him Bahá'u'lláh, the

Glory of God, and it was to him that the Báb sent his seals, his pen and papers.

Bahá'u'lláh gave the full weight of his prestige to the Cause of the Báb. He was too influential a figure to be ignored and on more than one occasion he challenged the clergy to refute him, but they were unequal to the task and resorted to those same methods which have ever been used by the opposers of truth.

Hearing that Mullá Ḥusayn, with three hundred of his companions, had sought refuge in a deserted shrine, and that an expedition had been despatched against them, Bahá'u'lláh set out to share their fortunes. On the way he was arrested and taken to Ámul. The mob, instigated by the clergy, clamoured for blood, and in order to appease them the Governor decided to inflict some punishment on Bahá'u'lláh's companions. Bahá'u'lláh offered himself as a scapegoat, and was bastinadoed.

On July 9th, 1850, the gentle and radiant Báb was executed. The Bábís were hunted down and done to death. Bahá'u'lláh was their only champion, the only one to whom they could look for moral and spiritual encouragement.

But now an incident occurred which gave the clergy and the officials the excuse they were looking for. Two young men, half demented by despair, resolved to avenge their martyred friends, and made an attempt on the life of the Sháh. Their mental condition was such that they loaded their pistols with shot quite incapable of killing a man. They were summarily dealt with, but the hue and cry was raised that here was proof of a deadly menace to the state. A campaign of extermination was begun.

Bahá'u'lláh at this time was staying at a summer resort near the capital. Declining the offers of friends to hide him, he set out to meet the Sháh. He was arrested and brought before a tribunal which recognized his innocence. Nevertheless he was taken—on foot—to Ṭihrán and thrown into a filthy underground dungeon, occupied by thieves and murderers. He wrote of this experience:

> 'No pen can depict that place, nor any tongue describe its loathsome smell. Most of these men had neither clothes nor bedding to lie on. God alone knoweth what befell Us in that most foul-smelling and gloomy place!'[7]

It was in this dark and airless prison, while loaded down with chains, that Bahá'u'lláh received the first intimations of his mission. He describes how he resolved that upon gaining his freedom he would *arise, . . . and undertake, with the utmost vigor, the task of regenerating* the Bábí community.

> 'One night, in a dream, these exalted words were heard on every side: "Verily, We shall render Thee victorious by Thyself and by Thy Pen. Grieve Thou not for that which hath befallen Thee, neither be Thou afraid, for Thou art in safety. Erelong will God raise up the treasures of the earth—men who will aid Thee through

Thyself and through Thy Name, wherewith God
hath revived the hearts of such as have recognized Him." ' [8]

But the time was not yet ripe for a declaration.
Upon leaving the prison, Bahá'u'lláh was deprived
of all his possessions, and with his family and a few
friends, was banished beyond the confines of his
native land. It was hoped that the journey to
Baghdád, undertaken in the depths of winter,
through bleak and mountainous country, would
result in his death and oblivion. But none knew of
his experience in the prison.

Having recovered from the effects of the journey,
Bahá'u'lláh began to revive and consolidate the
Bábís, a number of whom had gathered in Baghdád.
His half brother, Ṣubḥ-i-Azal, opposed him and
claimed to be the successor of the Báb. Bahá'u'lláh,
preferring not to be the cause of dissension to an
already weakened community, left Baghdád for the
mountains of Sulaymáníyyih. There for two years,
as Christ in the wilderness, as Buddha in the Indian
forest, as Muḥammad in the fiery hills of Arabia, he
became prepared for his task. He describes how he
was often without food and shelter, and yet lived in
perfect happiness. *The one object of Our retirement
was to avoid becoming a subject of discord among the faithful, a source of disturbance unto Our companions, the
means of injury to any soul, or the cause of sorrow to any
heart. Beyond these, We cherished no other intention, and
apart from them, We had no end in view.* [9]

Yet even in this remote and unpopulated part, his fame began to spread. It was told that a man of unsurpassed wisdom and kindliness was to be found there, and gradually the story was heard in Baghdád.

The Bábís, deprived of his guidance and authority, had become divided and despondent. No sooner did they hear of the wise man of Sulaymáníyyih than they recognized their lost counsellor and friend, and immediately despatched a mission to seek him and beg him to return. Bahá'u'lláh answered their call.

He returned to Baghdád in 1856 and restored order and happiness to the Bábí community. They were indeed glad, after their trials without him, to recognize his authority. Azal, the victim of his own vanity, still plotted against him, but the Bábís had learnt to know their true guide, and Bahá'u'lláh protected his enemy from the results of his own intrigues.

The faith of the Báb was renewed and invigorated and many came to enlist from other ranks than those of Shí'ih Islám, which until then had provided the great majority of the believers.

During his stay in Baghdád, Bahá'u'lláh wrote three of his most important works. The *Book of Certitude* is a clear explanation of the scriptures of Judaism, Christianity and Islám. It is an answer to those who mock at revealed religion because of the many inexplicable statements found in its books; it is a challenge to the agnostic; it is a revelation to those who insist on a literal interpretation of the words of the Prophets. It sets forward the story of progressive revelation, and expounds the mystical unity of the world's great religions.

The Seven Valleys, written in answer to the request of a Ṣúfí leader, describes the journey of man to God and, as its title suggests, deals with the different stages in this journey. The first is the 'Valley of Search', in which '*the traveler abideth in every land and dwelleth in every region. In every face, he seeketh the beauty of the Friend; in every country he looketh for the Beloved. He joineth every company, and seeketh fellowship with every soul, that haply in some mind he may uncover the secret of the Friend, or in some face he may behold the beauty of the Loved One.*'[10] How plain is this condition in the world today. How plain it was in the first centuries of the Christian era when a host of mystery cults and new religions, providing for one or other of the spiritual needs of the age, were finally absorbed by the revelation of Jesus Christ, which provided for them all.

The urge today seems to be for self-assertion and development of the ego beyond healthy limits, and many movements, both within and without Christianity, have flourished by giving it scope. But the seventh valley is the '*state . . . of dying from self and living in God, and being poor in self and becoming rich in the Desired One.*'[11]

While walking upon the banks of the Tigris, Bahá'u'lláh would meditate upon God's nearness to man and man's remoteness from God, and upon the fundamental truth of all religion. He wrote the *Hidden Words*, which is regarded of surpassing beauty, even in the rich literature of Persia.

'O Son of Spirit! Burst thy cage asunder, and even as the phoenix of love, soar into the firmament of holiness. Renounce thyself and, filled with the spirit of mercy, abide in the realm of celestial sanctity.'[12]

'O Rebellious Ones! My forbearance hath emboldened you and My long-suffering hath made you negligent, in such wise that ye have spurred on the fiery charger of passion into perilous ways that lead unto destruction. Have ye thought Me heedless, or that I was unaware?'[13]

The fame of Bahá'u'lláh began to spread, and many came to ask the solution of difficult problems, and to seek spiritual guidance. But the envy and malice of the Shí'ih clergy were enkindled anew and they met to discuss effective ways of undermining his growing influence. One of their number was commissioned to visit Bahá'u'lláh and to demand convincing proof of the station of the Báb. He returned to say that he had found only truth and righteousness in Bahá'u'lláh and to bring a definite challenge. Bahá'u'lláh would produce any proof they might desire, if they would afterwards accept his authority. The offer was not accepted.

Representations were now made to the Sháh to open negotiations with the Sultán of Turkey for the removal of Bahá'u'lláh further from the Persian frontier. After some time, the order came for his second banishment, to Constantinople.

The Bábís gathered sadly and tearfully to bid farewell to their loved counsellor. There, in the Najíbíyyih garden outside Baghdád, Bahá'u'lláh declared himself to be the one promised by the Báb, 'He Whom God shall manifest'. This was the twenty-first of April, 1863.

They received his statement with joy and reverence. Their sadness vanished, their trials and sufferings became triumphs; their vision was vindicated. 'He Whom God shall manifest' had at last appeared and the new age of mankind would surely be established. Henceforward the Faith of the Báb would be the Bahá'í Faith, and its followers Bahá'ís.

From Constantinople, after four months, Bahá'u'lláh was sent to Adrianople. There he made a public declaration of his mission and announced his revelation to be the one heralded by the Báb. There were written some of the famous 'Letters To The Kings', manuscripts in which the principles of justice are stressed and a plan of collective security outlined.* There also he suffered further from the hatred of Azal, who tried to poison him and then to have him assassinated.

In 1868 Bahá'u'lláh and his companions were sent into a yet more distant exile, this time to the Holy Land. To 'Akká, at the foot of Mount Carmel, they came by the will of their enemies, thus fulfilling the

* Among those addressed were: the Sháh, the Grand Vizier of Turkey, the Tsar, Queen Victoria, the German Emperor, Napoleon III, the Pope, the Presidents of the American Republics.[14]

prophecies of the Bible and the Qur'án. Here, under dreadful conditions, they lived for some years. Later, restrictions were somewhat relaxed and Bahá'u'lláh went to live at Bahjí, a short distance away. It was in this place that Edward Granville Browne, Fellow of Pembroke College, Cambridge, was received by Bahá'u'lláh. The account of the interview is the only one left by a westerner.

'The face of him on whom I gazed I can never forget, though I cannot describe it. Those piercing eyes seemed to read one's very soul; power and authority sat on that ample brow; while the deep lines on the forehead and face implied an age which the jet-black hair and beard flowing down in indistinguishable luxuriance almost to the waist seemed to belie. No need to ask in whose presence I stood, as I bowed myself before one who is the object of a devotion and love which kings might envy and emperors sigh for in vain!

'A mild dignified voice bade me be seated, and then continued:

"Praise be to God that thou hast attained! . . . Thou hast come to see a prisoner and an exile. . . . We desire but the good of the world and the happiness of the nations; yet they deem us a stirrer-up of strife and sedition worthy of bondage and banishment. . . . That all nations should become one in faith and all men as brothers; that the bonds of affection and unity between the sons of men should be strengthened; that diversity of religion should cease, and differences of race be

annulled—what harm is there in this? . . . Yet so
it shall be; these fruitless strifes, these ruinous
wars shall pass away, and the 'Most Great Peace'
shall come. . . . Do not you in Europe need this
also? Is not this that which Christ foretold? . . .
Yet do we see your kings and rulers lavishing
their treasures more freely on means for the
destruction of the human race than on that which
would conduce to the happiness of mankind. . . .
These strifes and this bloodshed and discord must
cease, and all men be as one kindred and one
family. . . . Let not a man glory in this, that he
loves his country; let him rather glory in this,
that he loves his kind. . . ."

'Such, so far as I can recall them, were the words
which, besides many others, I heard from Behá.
Let those who read them consider well with themselves whether such doctrines merit death and
bonds, and whether the world is more likely to gain
or lose by their diffusion.'[15]

Bahá'u'lláh left this mortal world in May 1892.
Mankind, shaken to its depths by forces which it can
neither control nor explain, may yet turn to him and
find the promised peace, assurance, and society-
building power which must characterize the Kingdom on earth.

The Branch

May 23rd, 1844, was a significant day in the
history of the world.

On that day in the eastern city of Shíráz, the Báb,

the morning star of the new day, made his declaration.

On that day in the western world, the first tele-
graphic message to be flashed along the wires was
sent from Baltimore to Washington. It read, 'What
hath God wrought.'

On that day was born 'Abdu'l-Bahá. He whom
many people, seeing only the perfect life and the
simple majesty, acclaimed as the Christ. They were
wrong; but not so wrong as those who saw only an
elderly man from the east.

How to write of him? It conveys little to say that
he was the eldest son of Bahá'u'lláh, the centre of
his Covenant, the exemplar of his teachings. Gentle
and wise, humorous and just, the 'father of the
poor', a healer to every sick one, a comforter to
every oppressed one, he was known to one and all
as the Master.

From the age of eight, until sixty-four, he
suffered persecution and oppression, the last forty
years being spent as a prisoner. His hardships began
when, in 1852, Bahá'u'lláh was thrown into the
dungeon in Ṭihrán. He accompanied the small band
of exiles on all their journeys, and entered the Great
Prison of 'Akká a young man of twenty-four. He
was to be released forty years later by the overthrow of those very forces which had been re-
sponsible for the persecutions and calumnies heaped
upon him and his beloved father.

Thereupon, in 1910, he set out to take the message of the new day to the western world. Egypt,

countries of Europe, and finally America were visited. He came to England twice, in 1911 and 1913, and the newspapers of the time prove that his visits were not unnoticed.

He chose for himself the title of 'Abdu'l-Bahá—the servant of Bahá—and by his life of service to humanity, showed what true religion meant.

All through the exiles and imprisonments, he was his father's constant companion and devoted son. His love for his father was boundless, but this did not deter him from showing constant care and attention to others; rather was it the source of his love for all people. When, shortly after the band of exiles had arrived in the prison of 'Akká, dysentery broke out, it was 'Abdu'l-Bahá who washed and fed and nursed them, until he too was stricken. He lived the life of Christ among the people, never caring for himself but always for them.

During the war of 1914–18 he was able, by the wise provisions which he had made, to feed the helpless people of Palestine, to keep corn from the destruction of the Turks and to provide General Allenby with food for his army when it eventually conquered the Holy Land.

The Turkish commander had threatened to crucify 'Abdu'l-Bahá on Mount Carmel, but the prompt action of the British Government averted the tragedy. Through the energy of Lady Blomfield, a prominent member of the Bahá'í community in England, a telegram was despatched from the War Office instructing General Allenby to 'extend every protection ... to 'Abdu'l-Bahá, his family and friends when the British march on Haifa'. Allenby's reply a few days later was to the effect, 'have today taken Palestine notify the world 'Abdu'l-Bahá is safe'. The details of this incident, together with letters from the officials concerned, are found in Lady Blomfield's book, *The Chosen Highway*.[16]

'Abdu'l-Bahá loved people to be happy, and he, more than any other, was the cause of their happiness. He saw immediately the need and condition of every soul and knew how to answer it. In his presence prejudices and differences evaporated, and only unity remained. Jews, Christians, Muḥammadans, Hindus, East and West, old and young, rich and poor, white and coloured, all were gathered together in the radiance of his universal spirit. He penetrated beneath the forms and creeds and names; membership of a church or society meant little to him. His only standard was the degree of striving to efface the self and come nearer to the divine perfection. '*Light is good in whatsoever lamp it shines,*' he would say, and in the visitors' book at Wandsworth Prison he wrote, '*The greatest prison is the prison of self.*'

Throughout his journeys in the west he addressed all kinds of societies, clubs, churches, giving to each encouragement in whatever they were doing for the betterment of mankind, but always stressing the oneness of humanity. He admitted no distinction of religion, colour, nation or class. The human heart was, to him, the home of God, and the exterior circumstances mattered little.

B

In spite of his sixty years of exile and imprisonment, educated only by his father's company and the holy books, such as the Bible and the Qur'án, he mixed naturally with scientists, economists, business men, educators, answering their questions and displaying a knowledge which no schooling could have given.

People tried to shower him with gifts. Flowers or fruit he would accept and distribute among his friends—those assembled at the time. Money, or valuable gifts, he did not accept. '*I came for the hearts,*' he would say.

By the provisions of Bahá'u'lláh's will, 'Abdu'l-Bahá was appointed sole interpreter of the Writings, and his word has the same validity as Bahá'u'lláh's own. He explained and amplified the teachings and his recorded talks and written letters form a large part of Bahá'í scripture.

He left his earthly frame in 1921, making provision in his Will and Testament for the future administration of the Faith in a manner (already outlined by Bahá'u'lláh) which is recognized to be unique, and which has preserved its unity in the face of tests and opposition. Today there is no Bahá'í sect, neither is there any priesthood, ritual or adopted creed.

Rather has the Faith forged ahead under the leadership of its appointed Guardian, Shoghi Effendi, winning to its ranks people of all races, classes, religious backgrounds, in all parts of the world, weathering persecution and establishing its Administrative Order on a universal foundation.

CHAPTER II

OUR PLACE IN HISTORY

HISTORY is too often thought of in the manner of '1066 And All That'. 'The Story Of Mankind' is its real name.

The series of events which is usually presented under the guise of 'history of a period', is but the outward sign of an inward process. That process, 'Abdu'l-Bahá teaches, is growth. The history of mankind is the story of his growth, and relates his activities in the various stages of development through which he has passed. These activities in turn tell—to those who recognize the process of growth in human society—what stage of development has been reached.

For instance, the great movement in Europe known as the Renaissance may be recognized as the period of transition from adolescence to youth of the people concerned. It is not just something that happened after the 'middle ages' because the Turks sacked Byzantium. It is the outward sign of a crucial moment in the growing up of the people of Europe, and has far deeper and earlier origins than the conquest of a city.

Similarly the disorder of the twentieth century is not to be attributed to the industrial revolution, the

Treaty of Versailles, capitalism or any single factor. It too is the outward effect of an inner crisis in human growth.

If we can visualize this process of growth, we may perhaps understand the true nature of our own times.

Now we must not expect to find the growth of mankind proceeding in a straight line; the world doesn't work like that. There is a law of rise and fall, of summer and winter, in human growth, just as there is in the world of nature. Periods of rest are needed just as much as periods of activity, but the living thing goes on growing all the time. We must remember this, and remember too that man's development has not been uniform; it has not taken place simultaneously all over the world. Great civilizations have arisen in the past, comparable (some would say preferable) to our own. So that when we say the development of man was from one stage to another, we cannot say that all mankind has made these changes at the same time.

We are therefore entitled to ask: Why has this development taken place at all? Why has it taken place at different times in different parts of the world? In the answer to these two questions we shall find the answer to the challenge of the twentieth century.

2

The first question is answered by the emphasis which the Bahá'í Faith places on purpose in history.

(Purpose in creation, if you like; history being the story of how that purpose is accomplished.) History is a process of development towards a definite goal, and is not merely the record of opposed groups fighting each other in hostile surroundings. Men have always had such a conception as is proved by our scripture, poetry and philosophy. Kant wrote in his essay on *Eternal Peace*: 'The history of the human race, viewed as a whole, may be regarded as the realization of a hidden plan of nature to bring about a political constitution, internally and externally perfect, as the only state in which all the capacities implanted by her in mankind can be fully developed.'[17]

'. . . realization of a hidden plan . . .'; there is the description of history. Just as the growth of a tree is the realization of a plan, hidden within the seed, to produce fruit, so the story of man is the realization of a plan, hidden within his own potential nature, to produce . . . what?

For thousands of years men have had the vision of a great day when 'they shall beat their swords into ploughshares', when 'the earth shall be full of the knowledge of its Lord', when there will be real brotherhood, the kingdom of God on earth. 'Thy kingdom come' was once a realistic and confident cry. Now that it has lost, or is losing its practical meaning, the astonishing announcement comes from Bahá'u'lláh, '*This is the Day*.' He declares that the vision which we have preserved for so long is a true one, and the goal of history is now to be reached.

That goal is not an end in itself, but only the gateway to something higher than has been known before. That goal is world brotherhood, or World Order. And World Order is the outward sign of the coming of age of the human race. Just as the tree, when it reaches the fruit-bearing stage, has the longest and most useful part of its life before it, so man, now that he is approaching maturity, stands at the threshold of the longest and most splendid era of his existence.

This World Order will not be established by any magical or arbitrary act, but must be attained by the human race through a painful transition from youth to manhood. *We are in that state of transition now.*

The period is painful and unsettled because, like most young people approaching maturity, we cling to the passions and prejudices, the heedlessness and irresponsibility of youth, when all the forces of the soul are pressing on to achieve their full inheritance.

Our view of history, then, is of a natural process of growth, which aims at bringing man, the individual and the community, to maturity, so that the potentialities latent within him may be fully manifested. Those potentialities are, individually, 'the image of God', and socially 'the Kingdom of God on earth'.

3

We now come to our second question. Why have civilizations risen, and fallen, at different times in different parts of the world?

The egoistic theory of special race quality, shouted so loudly in this century, quickly fails under inquiry. The theory of special environment also fails. We must look for some other factor to provide our answer.[18]

Modern scholarship recognizes that 'society'—a condition of group living—existed before man emerged on to the stage of history. This is in keeping with the teaching of Bahá'u'lláh and the Book of Genesis. Both teachings—Bahá'u'lláh specifically and Genesis circumstantially—tell that the stage was set for man before his actual appearance. The theory of evolution upholds this theme, and it is undoubtedly true.[19]

'Society' is necessary to man, and acts upon his inner consciousness as soil acts upon a seed. It provides the necessary environment for growth, enables latent powers to be manifested in a new form, and acts as the perpetual background, the impersonal Mother, in which the living thing may take root, and from which it may, from time to time, draw new life.

In the natural world these periods of new life occur rhythmically and through the agency of something entirely apart from either the seed or the soil. Through the unfailing appearance of the sun, the seasons of the earth proceed in orderly sequence.

So it is with man. Man is the seed, society is the soil. What is the sun? Bahá'u'lláh states clearly, emphatically and repeatedly, that the sun which shines upon the soul of man and brings new life to his spirit, is religion. Its shining may be strong and vital, or weak and feeble, like the physical sun. But in either case the condition of society is dependent; it is either vigorous and progressive, or disintegrating.

This principle of rise and fall, of summer and winter, is found in all things. The growth of man is no exception to it. From inactivity he is stimulated to mental and spiritual action, and then goes back to rest, only to be reawakened later, to take up the struggle again. Civilization emerges from the darkness and is followed by a decline, followed in turn by a renaissance.

The renewal of vigour in the human world is accomplished by the unfailing appearance 'of a succession of Great Souls especially appointed and empowered for the task. These Great Souls, who are men and yet more than men, are the key figures of history: it is they who inspire the onward movement of mankind and determine the manifold phases of human progress and enlightenment.'[20]

They are the revealers of religion and the founders of civilization.

Christendom was built on the spiritual teachings of Christ. Islám was the civilization impelled by Muḥammad. The great Israelitish culture which produced Solomon arose on the revelation of Moses. Through Zoroaster came the spiritual force which found expression in the Persian era of Cyrus and Darius. Krishna and Buddha have revealed the truth and released the impulse which has united millions in the Orient under common codes of morals and behaviour.

The fact that civilization has arisen upon the spiritual impulse imparted by a revealer of religion, is one of those obvious truths which has hardly ever occurred to most of us, and even less often has been presented to us in school.* Bahá'u'lláh stresses it and unveils the historical plan, the realization of which is the purpose of *all* the Prophets, or Manifestations of God. They are the appearances of the spiritual 'Sun', at different times and under different names, but imbued with the same power and serving the same purpose.

Just as the renewal of the seasons is dependent upon the appearance of the sun, so the renewal of civilization is dependent upon the appearance of the Manifestation of God. The 'return' of the sun is the first essential of continuity, a teaching upheld by the Bible and the Gospel, in spite of the exclusive claims of the church. Buddha Siddartha is one of a line of Buddhas. Krishna stated that he (the spirit he mani-

---

* This subject has been insufficiently studied. The author does not now state (though he believes) that all civilization is due to religion; the circumstantial proofs are insufficient, though psychological and anthropological evidence is compelling. It is known that other civilizations—Egyptian, Greek, Central American— have been profoundly conditioned by their religion, but (for instance) the origins of much of Greek religion are lost in the antiquity of Crete and may now be so for ever, due to the warfare round Knossos; also the extent of the influence of Judaism on Greek thought is not properly known; what did Socrates bring after his studies with the Jewish sages?

It *is* stated that every founder of a world religion has also been a founder of civilization.

fested) appeared from time to time. The scriptures
of all the great Faiths give promise of a great and
wonderful time to come, which is always associated
with the appearance of a new Messiah.

Here is the explanation of the rise and fall of
civilization. The appearance of the Manifestation is
the heart beat of society, the force which causes the
pulse of organic humanity to throb. It is the same
principle which is seen in the surge and resurge of
the tides, in sleeping and waking, in summer and
winter.

The appearance of this Great Being, Bahá'u'lláh
teaches, although it takes place approximately once
in a thousand years, is not according to any fixed
time, but is dependent upon the condition of society.
When humanity is in its darkest winter, then the new
Sun appears above the horizon, slowly and with
gentle warmth at first. It rises to its meridian
splendour and then declines, leaving the traces of a
great day and also leaving the process of growth so
much more advanced, for each beat of the pulse of
history sends man farther along his path of development.

Recall that by the time the splendour of Judaism
was faded, its greatness corrupted by superstition
and hypocrisy, when the glory of Greece was gone,
when the iron fist of Rome dominated the world, a
new sunrise was urgently needed to save humanity
from perpetual barbaric winter. Jesus, the Sun of
Christianity, rose above the horizon and without
material force or support infused such a spirit of

devotion and vigour into a few poor people, as to enable them to triumph over the social science of the age. This spirit it was that carried the light of civilization through the period of Roman decadence and finally impressed itself upon the world through the agency of Constantine.

By the seventh century civilization was again dying; the 'dark ages' had set in in Europe. At this time Muḥammad appeared.

The Arab race was composed of scattered tribes, barbarous, ignorant, disunited, spending their time and energy in inter-tribal wars in which the victor carried off the women of the vanquished and added them to the already lengthy list of his wives. They worshipped idols and had only the most primitive social ideas.

Sixty years after Muḥammad they were a strong united nation, progressing in civilization in the brotherhood of Islám. They learnt and believed the story of the Bible and the Gospel, and they acknowledged the one God. 'There is no God but God, and Muḥammad is His Prophet.' They raised the status of women* and built a strong, organic social order. They became world leaders in medicine, mathematics and astronomy; they performed major operations, with alcohol as an anaesthetic, while be-

* Muḥammad permitted a believer to marry four wives, on *condition* that he treated them with equal justice! He gave them certain rights in the home, of property and administration, and greatly improved their lot. The practices of Muslims in later times are no fairer standard of judgment than would be the slums of Christian countries for an appraisal of the Gospel.

nighted Christians paid for priestly incantations to cure them of their diseases. They introduced the modern numerical system without which modern calculations would be impossible. (Try to make out your income tax in Roman figures.) They created an architectural form which ranks with the most beautiful of the world; they extended their culture as far west as Spain and as far east as India. Baghdád became the centre of the world, not only in riches, but in art and learning. They united in one fellowship such varied peoples as Arabs, Turks, Hindus, Egyptians, Moors, Persians. They preserved the learning and philosophy of Greece which the early Church had tried to destroy. They carried the classical knowledge over the period of the dark ages, vastly enriched it and then, through the medium of their universities such as Cordova, through the crusaders and merchants, sent it westwards and gave that fresh impetus to Christendom which we call the Renaissance, and from which our civilization dates.

Thus was the divine plan carefully tended; thus was the sleeper awakened.

'Abdu'l-Bahá speaks of the effect produced by the passing of the sun northwards and southwards across the equator, and then continues:

'In like manner when the Holy Manifestation of God, who is the Sun of the world of His creation, shines upon the worlds of spirits, of thoughts, and of hearts, then the spiritual spring and new life appear, the power of the wonderful springtime becomes visible, and marvellous benefits are apparent. As you have observed, at the time of the appearance of each Manifestation of God, extraordinary progress has occurred in the world of minds, thoughts, and spirits.' [21]

It is through this succession of spiritual seasons that mankind slowly unfolds the potentialities within it.

Those small groups of people living on the earth today, who have not been subject to these successive impulses—the 'backward races'—are examples of the impotence of man to develop without them. All 'civilized' peoples have come under their influence, either directly, as in the case of European pagans and Jesus Christ; or indirectly as in the case of decadent Christendom and Islám, which caused a renewal of Christianity in Europe.

Past civilizations have necessarily been localized, for invention and discovery have never before attained their present degree. The world was not explored until recent years and universality was a physical impossibility. Oceans, mountain ranges and deserts successfully divided the human race.

It is a basic teaching of Bahá'u'lláh that the revelation of religion is appropriate to the time and condition in which it is made. To all parts of the world, at some time or times, has been revealed the Truth (absolute in its essence), but stated according to the need, condition, and capacity of the occasion. Today the world is in urgent need of another Manifestation of God with an all-embracing message and a power that can reconcile the opposing factions into which the old era has crystallized.

Bahá'u'lláh fills this need. It is his specific mission. He is the Focal Point of this day, from which emanates the new spirit and the new plan for the further unfoldment of history. He speaks to the whole human race; his revelation is not specifically for any people or country, but for the whole world. His spiritual teachings confirm all previous revelation and his administrative institutions are designed to cope with world affairs as well as with individual activities.

He assures us that this is the Promised Day, the millennium, the day of God anticipated by people through all ages, the day promised in all the holy books.

What hath God wrought, indeed! Only the majestic utterance of Bahá'u'lláh can do justice to this magnificent theme.

'This is the King of Days, the Day that hath seen the coming of the Best-beloved, Him Who through all eternity hath been acclaimed the Desire of the World.'[22]

'Through the movement of Our Pen of glory We have, at the bidding of the omnipotent Ordainer, breathed a new life into every human frame and instilled into every word a fresh potency. All created things proclaim the evidences of this world-wide regeneration.'[23]

The history of the last hundred years is only intelligible in the light which Bahá'u'lláh sheds upon it.

The terrific crescendo of scientific and intellectual progress has been matched by a decline in moral standards and values, so that we are totally unfitted to manage the gigantic forces at our disposal; they are turned towards destruction, in a futile attempt to preserve the youthful way of life in the age of maturity.

History is repeating itself on a larger scale; the season has come round again, springtime, when the rigid grip of winter fails before the rising sun. The destruction of Jerusalem, the sack of Rome, the fall of Assyria, is being re-enacted on a universal stage with the awful proficiency of modern destructive power, and uncurbed national hatreds, magnifying the intensity a thousandfold. But it *is* springtime—and for all mankind. Certain bad old things are going, unfettered national sovereignty and class prejudice, to name but two.

The old way of seeing things, and doing things, is passing violently. But destruction is not the whole picture. Far from it. In the midst of the clamour and tumult, the Bahá'í Faith stands, not as the straw for the drowning man, but the impregnable fortress which '*storms of human strife are powerless to undermine*', the fortress in which the individual, reborn, with a new spirit, remains undaunted through the uproar and finds, through a sense of world citizenship, the urge to serve and live according to the new principles. Strong in some countries, weak in others, repressed in others, insignificant in others, generally poor in numbers and resources, it serves the whole race in the same way that 'the contemptible sect of the Nazarene' served a part of it when the Roman world toppled about its ears.

*   *   *

There is in human nature, spiritual and intellectual potentiality for development of a higher and higher form of social order. The form itself reaches its ultimate size and shape with the boundaries of the planet, that is in a World Order, but development within that final commonwealth is unlimited.

The process of history, then, is in the very nature of things; it is the realization of the inner potentialities of man himself, just as the growth of a tree is the realization of the potentialities within the seed; an organic process, following the cycles determined by the appearance of the Manifestation of God.

From family life to tribal life, to city state, to provinces, kingdoms, nations, the story has unfolded, and now enters its greatest climax.

This is the unique distinction of the present day. Out of the chaos and destruction the ultimate form of human society is slowly and painfully emerging. Mankind is coming of age.

CHAPTER III

PURIFICATION

THE mature spirit of man must have adequate channels for its expression. The present world provides only the institutions of adolescence and youth: competitive nationalism, social and economic classes, party politics and sectarian religion.

New and universal institutions are needed. A world economic system; world government; a world society; a true corporate state of mankind.

Such an order, however, can only be achieved by mature human beings; it cannot successfully be imposed on adolescents, moral or intellectual. If men are greedy, selfish, without social conscience, no system will make life worth living. Before, therefore, examining the realistic teachings of Bahá'u'lláh on world organization, let us see what hope there is to still the passions and hatreds, and change the self-seeking and moral darkness of our generation, into true fellowship and light.

Who can change a human heart? Who can galvanize a slothful spirit into radiant activity in the path of spiritual growth?

Jesus Christ could. Today the church cannot. Muḥammad could. Today Islám cannot. None of the historic religious systems show any signs of provoking a world renaissance, or even of producing so great a figure as St. Francis. Judaism, Christianity and Islám are concerned with preserving their own forms and ceremonies; Buddhism and Hinduism appear lost in the intricacies of their own mysticism. A host of new sects and cults, 'violent fires' which 'soon burn out themselves', invade the ranks of orthodoxy; atheism and materialism take their toll, from all religions, of those who will not accept blindly or bear with apathy.

Where then lies salvation? Who can purify religion from its accumulated dust and cobwebs? Who can answer the cry of the disillusioned millions, those 'hungry sheep' who 'look up and are not fed'?

2

In the Bahá'í Faith there is no priesthood, ritual or sacrament. The elected bodies cannot adopt articles of faith or formulate a creed, and the scriptures are preserved in their original written form.

Faced with such drastic removal of the familiar trappings of religion, many people ask 'Well, how does it work?' 'What do you do?' The reader is referred to Chapter VIII, where an outline is given of the Bahá'í Administrative Order. At the moment we are concerned with purifying religion of its superstitions, prejudices and irrational teachings.

The first religious principle restated and emphasized by Bahá'u'lláh is that of manifestation. The nature of the divinity attributed to the Founders of religion has been the cause of conflict and atheism, so it is important to have this matter clarified.

God does not incarnate Himself. He never assumes the form of a human temple and walks upon the earth.

This teaching is, of course, in direct conflict with the official teachings of the Christian church. But these teachings themselves, on this particular matter, cannot be upheld by the sayings of Jesus Christ. The doctrine of the Trinity, embodying the incarnation and the three-fold nature of the Godhead, was officially adopted by the Council of Nicaea, A.D. 325. Jesus Christ never claimed equality with God; his whole life and teaching was one of dependence on 'The Father'. He did claim however, to reveal God to man. '. . . *he that hath seen me hath seen the Father* . . .'[24]

Bahá'u'lláh writes on this matter:

'To every discerning and illumined heart it is evident that God, the unknowable Essence, the Divine Being, is immeasurably exalted beyond every human attribute such as corporeal existence, ascent and descent, egress and regress . . . He is, and hath ever been, veiled in the ancient eternity of His Essence, and will remain in His Reality everlastingly hidden from the sight of men. . . . He standeth exalted beyond and above all separation and union, all proximity and remoteness. . . .'[25]

'From time immemorial, He, the Divine Being,

hath been veiled in the ineffable sanctity of His exalted Self, and will everlastingly continue to be wrapt in the impenetrable mystery of His unknowable Essence. . . .'[26]

'The door of the knowledge of the Ancient of Days being thus closed in the face of all beings, He, the Source of infinite grace . . . hath caused those luminous Gems of Holiness to appear out of the realm of the spirit, in the noble form of the human temple, and be made manifest unto all men, that they may impart unto the world the mysteries of the unchangeable Being and tell of the subtleties of His imperishable Essence. . . . All the Prophets of God, His well-favoured, His holy and chosen Messengers are, without exception, the bearers of His names and the embodiments of His attributes. . . . These Tabernacles of Holiness, these primal Mirrors which reflect the Light of unfading glory, are but expressions of Him Who is the Invisible of the Invisibles.'[27]

'Abdu'l-Bahá never failed to produce a perfect analogy or metaphor to make clear abstruse or subtle points. He explains the station of the Manifestations by the reflection of the sun in a perfect mirror, which, when polished and faced directly towards the sun, faithfully reflects its light and heat, shape, radiance and other attributes. The Manifestation of God is the perfect Mirror, reflecting all the power and knowledge of God, the Sun of Truth. If one looks into the glass mirror and says, there is the sun, it is the truth. Similarly if one looks at the Manifestation of God and says, there is

God, it is the truth.* But the phenomenal sun does not leave its station in the heavens to inhabit the mirror; neither does God, the all-pervading spirit of the universe, constrain His Being to the limited capacity of a human temple.

The Guardian of the Bahá'í Faith, emphasizing this cardinal point, writes, 'The human temple that has been made the vehicle of so overpowering a Revelation must, if we be faithful to the tenets of our Faith, ever remain entirely distinguished from that "innermost Spirit of Spirits" and "eternal Essence of Essences"—that invisible yet rational God Who, however much we extol the divinity of His Manifestations on earth, can in no wise incarnate His infinite, His unknowable, His incorruptible and all-embracing Reality in the concrete and limited frame of a mortal being. Indeed, the God Who could so incarnate His own reality would, in the light of the teachings of Bahá'u'lláh, cease immediately to be God. So crude and fantastic a theory of Divine incarnation is as removed from, and incompatible with, the essentials of Bahá'í belief as are the no less inadmissible pantheistic and anthropomorphic conceptions of God—both of which the utterances of Bahá'u'lláh emphatically repudiate and the fallacy of which they expose.'[28]

Bahá'u'lláh teaches, then, that God is unknowable to man, except through His Manifestations, His Christs, who appear in every age *out of the realm of the spirit, in the noble form of the human temple* to reveal

* '... he that hath seen me hath seen the Father ...'

to man's developing understanding the mysteries of the *'unchangeable Being'*.[29]

This is a far more rational statement than the general Christian Theology, and is upheld by the holy books of all the world religions. It denies nothing in the Bible, the Gospel, the Qur'án and is acceptable to the modern mind.

It also leads directly to another fact, specifically confirmed by Bahá'u'lláh and finding wider and wider acceptance among thinking people, namely that God has revealed Himself to men more than once during recorded history. The doctrine of the 'only begotten Son' is another dogma which finds no support in the statements of Jesus Christ. On the contrary, previous Revelations (those of Moses and Abraham) are recognized, and others foretold for the future. The exclusive claims of the Church to salvation and entrance to the 'Kingdom of heaven' fail before this truth. By it, too, man is relieved of the necessity of applying laws given nearly two thousand years ago, to modern conditions. In actual fact, mankind has already taken this relief in defiance of the Church; in the matter of divorce for instance.

3

Bahá'u'lláh teaches that revelation is progressive, and that each Manifestation of God answers the need of his time. This need has two voices: one, crying for spiritual food, satisfaction of the inner life, 'knowledge of God', faith, is always answered in the same way, through spiritual teachings, an outpouring of love, and a renewal of the soul's vigour. The other voice cries for laws to regulate excesses, abrogation of outworn customs, and organization of daily affairs.

Both cries are answered. Moses revived the faith of the captive Israelites and gave them laws. Jesus gave to drink *'of that water which is life indeed'*; but the rigid law of the Sabbath was abrogated, and to correct the excesses of the time, divorce was forbidden. Muḥammad gave his people faith in Alláh, and also laws and regulations which proved of the greatest benefit. Bahá'u'lláh again pours out the 'water of life', in answer to our cry, and also gives us laws and regulations for modern affairs.

'Know of a certainty that in every Dispensation the light of Divine Revelation has been vouchsafed to men in direct proportion to their spiritual capacity. Consider the sun. How feeble its rays the moment it appeareth above the horizon. How gradually its warmth and potency increase as it approacheth its zenith, enabling meanwhile all created things to adapt themselves to the growing intensity of its light. How steadily it declines until it reacheth its setting point. Were it all of a sudden to manifest the energies latent within it, it would no doubt cause injury to all created things. . . . In like manner, if the Sun of Truth were suddenly to reveal, at the earliest stages of its manifestation, the full measure of the potencies which the providence of the Almighty hath bestowed upon it, the earth of human understanding would waste away and be consumed; for men's hearts would neither sustain the intensity of its revelation, nor be able to mirror forth the radiance of its light. Dismayed and overpowered, they would cease to exist.'[30]

The Bahá'í revelation is no exception to this basic principle. 'It should also be borne in mind that, great as is the power manifested by this Revelation and however vast the range of the Dispensation its Author has inaugurated, it emphatically repudiates the claim to be regarded as the final revelation of God's will and purpose for mankind. To hold such a conception of its character and functions would be tantamount to a betrayal of its cause and a denial of its truth. It must necessarily conflict with the fundamental principle which constitutes the bedrock of Bahá'í belief, the principle that religious truth is not absolute but relative, that Divine Revelation is orderly, continuous and progressive and not spasmodic or final. Indeed, the categorical rejection by the followers of the Faith of Bahá'u'lláh of the claim to finality which any religious system inaugurated by the Prophets of the past may advance is as clear and emphatic as their own refusal to claim that same finality for the Revelation with which they stand identified.'[31]

4

There is only one religion.

There is but one God, by whatever name He is called. There is but one human race. There can be but one religion. But this one religion has many Speakers, and many expressions.

The life and progress of man are dependent upon the Word of God. In past times the human race was divided by oceans, mountain ranges, forests, deserts, all the physical barriers which modern invention has just succeeded in surmounting. This is one reason why there have been many revealers of the Word of God; so that all mankind should receive it.*

There is another reason. Religion becomes corrupt; it loses its early vigour and degenerates into institutions with no spiritual force to energize the inner life of man. Therefore it must be renewed and purified. This is accomplished through the influence of a Messiah ... another Speaker.

There is yet another reason. Man, through successive seasons of civilization and decline, grows in understanding and social capacity. He therefore needs, from time to time, a further measure of that essential, real truth which is both the food of his spirit and the energy of his new civilization. This truth is revealed by a divine messenger.

Bahá'u'lláh teaches:

(1) that religious revelation is progressive;
(2) that old forms and institutions must give way to new ones;
(3) that revelation is according to the need and capacity of the time.

* There is no known society without religion. 'Savage civilizations' have very definite religious teachings, well adapted to their circumstances.

The first teaching is upheld by the Bible, the Gospel and the Qur'án, by the Bhagavad Gita and the Gospel of Buddha. The Old Testament contains the story of successive revelation up to the beginning of the Christian era. The Gospel confirms the teaching of the Old Testament, fulfils many of its prophecies and emphatically renews the promise of another Messiah (or the 'return' of *the* Messiah). The Qur'án confirms both the Old Testament and the New, and again renews this promise.

The second teaching is a recognized requirement of all phases of life, but a strange and quite unfounded exception is given to religious institutions. Why? They too are mortal, and must give way to new ones. Jesus Christ taught this; '*Heaven and earth shall pass away, but my words shall not pass away.*'[32] (Heaven is the place where the sun resides—the synagogue, church, mosque or temple from which the light of religion shines; earth is the recipient of the light—the social order. Both shall pass away; but the light shall not pass away.)

Jesus Christ also supports the third teaching, that religious revelation is according to the capacity and the need. '*I have yet many things to say unto you, but ye cannot bear them now. Howbeit when he, the Spirit of truth, is come, he will guide you into all truth . . .*'[33] 'You cannot bear it now.' Surely if men are wise enough to educate their children according to this principle, God will do no less!

The true educator of man is the Founder of religion, who trains him in morals and the higher virtues and reveals to him his spiritual reality. All the Prophets have served this purpose. They have trained men in honesty, truthfulness, trustworthiness, reverence, modesty, civil obedience and self-sacrifice for others. *The essential teaching of all Religion is the same.*

But the names of the speakers are different; they apply spiritual truth differently to different conditions, and that is a great source of annoyance to conventional minds (not only in religion). Justice at one time was achieved by 'an eye for an eye and a tooth for a tooth', but that application today would be barbarous. At one time divorce was permitted, at another forbidden. When women were regarded as chattels and had no protection unless belonging to a man, polygamy was sanctioned.* In hot countries the eating of pork was forbidden. One day of the week must be kept free from work, so Muslims, Jews and Christians remain exclusive about this and keep Friday, Saturday and Sunday respectively.

The differences in religion are due to the different requirements of the times in which each revelation was made, and the enmity between religions is due to prejudice and ignorance.

'Know thou assuredly that the essence of all the Prophets . . . is one and the same. Their unity is absolute. God, the Creator saith: There is no distinction whatsoever among the Bearers of My

* It is believed by a large number of Christians that Jesus taught monogamy. Actually there is nothing about it in the Gospel and polygamy was practised among the early believers.

Message. They all have but one purpose; their secret is the same secret.' 'It is clear and evident, therefore, that any apparent variation in the intensity of their light is not inherent in the light itself, but should rather be attributed to the varying receptivity of an ever-changing world. Every Prophet Whom the Almighty and Peerless Creator hath purposed to send to the peoples of the earth hath been entrusted with a Message, and charged to act in a manner that would best meet the requirements of the age in which He appeared.'[34]

Here is a teaching, acceptable to reason, in accord with historical evidence, and, moreover, capable of removing religious enmity and of providing a basis for true spiritual brotherhood among all people.*

Confession, monastic life, ritual and priesthood are all forbidden in the Bahá'í Faith.

'The pious practices of the monks and priests among the people of His Holiness the Spirit (i.e. Christ)—upon Him is the peace of God and His glory!—are remembered before God; but, in this day, they must abandon solitude for open places, and engage in that which may profit both themselves and other men. We have conferred permission on them all to engage in matrimony, so that there may appear from them those who (i.e. children) may celebrate the praise of God, the Lord of the seen and unseen and the Lord of the lofty throne!'†

* For further discussion of the oneness of religion, see Chapter IV, Sect. 2.
† Bahá'u'lláh in *The Glad Tidings*.[35]

'It is not allowable to declare one's sins and transgressions before any man, inasmuch as this has not been, nor is, conducive to securing God's forgiveness and pardon. At the same time such confession before the creatures leads to one's humiliation and abasement, and God—exalted is His glory!—does not wish for the humiliation of His servants. Verily He is Compassionate and Beneficent!'*

Religion has indeed been purified. Bahá'u'lláh has purged it of ecclesiasticism, austerity, superstition and priestcraft. No longer is blind acceptance of a creed permissible; no longer may books be 'blacklisted'. The command is on all men to investigate independently, to seek the Truth through all available channels, science, art, work, worship, recreation, prayer, and meditation.

Clear from a fresh spring, religious truth is once again shaping the lives of men and guiding the destiny of the race. Religion has assumed a new meaning; it is no longer a weapon to intimidate the masses or a consolation for the fainthearted. It is a vibrant, compelling force, urging men on through love, to excel in 'The Divine Art of Living', whose master was 'Abdu'l-Bahá. He, the perfect Exemplar of the Bahá'í life, has set a standard far removed from the shoddy scandals, self-seeking and personal satisfactions of present-day society. Translating the law of Christ, 'that ye love one another', into everyday ethics, 'Abdu'l-Bahá has said that to live the life is:

* Bahá'u'lláh in *The Glad Tidings*.[35]

To be no cause of grief to anyone.

To be kind to all people and to love them with a pure spirit.

Should opposition or injury happen to us to bear it, to be as kind as ever we can be, and through all, to love the people. Should calamity exist in the greatest degree, to rejoice, for these things are the gifts and favours of God.

To be silent concerning the faults of others, to pray for them, and to help them, through kindness, to correct their faults.

To look always at the good and not at the bad. If a man has ten good qualities and one bad one, look at the ten and forget the one. And if a man has ten bad qualities and one good one, to look at the one and forget the ten.

Never to allow ourselves to speak one unkind word about another, even though that other be our enemy.

To do all our deeds in kindness.

To sever our hearts from ourselves and from the world.

To be humble.

To be servants of each other, and to know that we are less than anyone else.

To be as one soul in many bodies; for the more we love each other, the nearer we shall be to God; but to know that our love, our unity, our obedience must not be by confession, but of reality.

To act with cautiousness and wisdom.

To be truthful.

To be hospitable.

To be reverent.

To be a cause of healing for every sick one, a comforter for every sorrowful one, a pleasant water for every thirsty one, a heavenly table for every hungry one, a star to every horizon, a light for every lamp, a herald to everyone who yearns for the kingdom of God.

CHAPTER IV

PRINCIPLES OF WORLD ORDER

THE strength of an organic society depends upon the unity of its millions of diversified individuals in a common ideology, which must be excellently suited to the needs and conditions of that society. Bahá'u'lláh, inaugurating the world society of the human race, enunciated certain principles which form the mental and spiritual atmosphere of the new age. The degree to which these principles have permeated human consciousness is the gauge which shows our nearness to that World Order which they were designed to sustain.

As this chapter proceeds it will become apparent that all Bahá'u'lláh's principles have already made their mark on the world; some are acclaimed by the vast majority of the race and one or two, such as the equality of men and women, have become so intrinsic a part of the modern attitude as to be taken for granted.* But remember that they were proclaimed a hundred years ago, when they were either astounding or unintelligible or heretical to all but a few enlightened people.

'Abdu'l-Bahá wrote:

---

* At present this equality is only objective; very few men really recognize the essential equality of women.

'In every Dispensation the light of Divine Guidance has been focussed upon one central theme. . . . In this wondrous Revelation, this glorious century, the foundation of the Faith of God and the distinguishing feature of His Law, is the consciousness of the Oneness of Mankind.'[36]

This principle, around which all the others revolve, is confirmed by the findings of science. Anthropology has revealed to us our common ancestry; it has proved conclusively that the human race, though varying in colour, size and feature, is not made up of different kinds and species. Humanity is one, homo sapiens, Man. We are one people from the same origin and with the same history.

The ingenious theories of essential racial superiority, which many people hold, cannot survive investigation. Indeed they prove to be nothing more than expressions of national or racial conceit, when considered without prejudice or egoism. The best exposition of their falseness is found in A. J. Toynbee's *A Study of History*, volume 1, pages 205–271, where many authorities are invoked to support the argument. Here we quote two more.

Professor Dorsey in *Why We Behave Like Human Beings* writes: 'There is no known fact of human anatomy or physiology which implies that capacity for culture or civilization or intelligence inheres in this race or that type . . .' He then asks, very pertinently: 'What wave did the Anglo-Saxon ride in the days of Tut-ankh-Amen, or of Caesar, or of

William the Conqueror?' 'How "low" the savage European must have seemed to the Nile Valley African, looking north from his pyramid of Cheops!'[37]

Professor Hooton in *Up From the Ape* says that there is no fair basis for estimating the capacity of the present 'backward races' for civilization, and continues: 'What possibilities of cultural achievement would an educated Roman, living in Britain in the fourth century A.D., have attributed to the native inhabitants of that island? How much of "racial" or ethnic ability would Pericles have granted to contemporary Romans?'

Bahá'u'lláh proclaims in simple language:

'Ye are all the leaves of one tree, the drops of one ocean.'

This truth is implicit in all religious teaching, but it has never really been accepted; certainly not by Christian nations who are well known for their colour, national and class prejudices.

Bahá'u'lláh, as we have indicated, lays great emphasis upon it. It is the foundation of the world society, and has practical application to human affairs. 'Let there be no mistake. The principle of the Oneness of Mankind—the pivot round which all the teachings of Bahá'u'lláh revolve—is no mere outburst of ignorant emotionalism or an expression of vague and pious hope. Its appeal is not to be merely identified with a reawakening of the spirit of brotherhood and good-will among men, nor does

C

it aim solely at the fostering of harmonious co-operation among individual peoples and nations. Its implications are deeper, its claims greater than any which the Prophets of old were allowed to advance. Its message is applicable not only to the individual, but concerns itself primarily with the nature of those essential relationships that must bind all the states and nations as members of one human family. It does not constitute merely the enunciation of an ideal, but stands inseparably associated with an institution* adequate to embody its truth, demonstrate its validity, and perpetuate its influence. It implies an organic change in the structure of present-day society, a change such as the world has not yet experienced. It constitutes a challenge, at once bold and universal, to outworn shibboleths of national creeds—creeds that have had their day and which must, in the ordinary course of events as shaped and controlled by Providence, give way to a new gospel, fundamentally different from, and infinitely superior to, what the world has already conceived. It calls for no less than the reconstruction and the demilitarization of the whole civilized world—a world organically unified in all the essential aspects of its life, its political machinery, its spiritual aspiration, its trade and finance, its script and language, and yet infinite in the diversity of the national characteristics of its federated units.'[38]

* A World Legislature.

2

The oneness of religion, which has already been discussed in the preceding chapter, is an essential part of World Order, for until men are united spiritually, there can be no true brotherhood, nor any universally accepted authority. And both are essential to social order.

The 'Book' has been the authority in the past. The Qur'án for Islám, the Bible for Christendom.* But the Muslim nations (comprising some three hundred and fifty million people) will not accept the human interpretation of the Gospel in place of the Qur'án. Neither will Christian nations accept the Qur'án in place of the laws they themselves have evolved. This is but one instance of the difficulties in bringing about religious unity. We have yet to think of Buddhists and Hindus, each numbering hundreds of millions.

Bahá'u'lláh solves this problem. He asks none of the established religions to accept the laws and ordinances of one among them, neither does he leave us to fight it out among ourselves. In his own revelation he fulfils the hopes and promises of all previous religions, those promises recorded in their own scriptures. His Book of Laws has the same authority as the Ten Commandments or the Sermon on the Mount, and is acceptable to all religions.

Bahá'u'lláh shows how the teaching of a Mani-

* The Zend Avesta; the Vedas; the Bhagavad Gita, etc.

festation of God is divided into two parts. The spiritual principles which do not change, and social ordinances and decrees which vary with the growth of man. Various religious systems developing round the Person of their Founder, come into contact with other 'religions' which have grown in the same way, and because they see the outer differences, accentuated by differences of climate, occupation and clothing, conclude that they are actually different religions. The inevitable conclusion is that 'ours' is the only true one, thus making superficial differences into impassable barriers.

The Bahá'í recognizes all the world's 'Bibles' as having come from the same source, through a Manifestation of God. He can, therefore, meet the Buddhist, Hindu, Christian, Jew, Muslim, on a basis denied to members of more exclusive systems; and he can also meet them all at once and bring them into a relatedness which no social tact or diplomacy could achieve. Bahá'í communities, in fact, are drawn from all these backgrounds, as well as from the various sects into which the great religious systems have disintegrated.

Without denying what has gone before, and without 'lowering' one Manifestation in favour of another, the Truth revealed by Bahá'u'lláh is able to bring religious unity to a torn and divided race.

The guidance of God is given to man from age to age through His Christs. At one time the Christ is called Jesus, at another Buddha, at others Moses,

Muḥammad, Krishna, Bahá'u'lláh. *It is always the same Christ.* Just as the sun is called Monday, Tuesday, Wednesday; or March, April, May or 1970, 1971, 1972; it is always the same sun.

Whenever the truth and vigour of religion has become vitiated by spiritual apathy, and no longer sustains human relationships and progress, then a restatement and a further revelation is made. *'Whenever there is decay of righteousness . . . and there is exaltation of unrighteousness, then I myself come forth, for the protection of the good, for the destruction of evil-doers, for the sake of firmly establishing righteousness; I am born from age to age.'*[39] (Krishna.)

This is exactly what has happened in the world today. And just as the truth of Christ's word gleamed amidst a multitude of new sects and cults, so the brilliance of Bahá'u'lláh's revelation has touched to life numerous revival movements, new religious philosophies and departures from orthodoxy. But who today knows of the Mandeans, of the Essenes, of Marcion, of Mithra? Who today knows of Christ? *'The Hand of Omnipotence hath established His Revelation upon an unassailable, an enduring foundation.'*[40] This is true of all the Manifestations of God, since they all speak of the same God and reveal the same truth, according to the needs and capacities of the time.

3

The Abandonment of Prejudice and Superstition

Bahá'u'lláh includes among superstitions all those

beliefs which have no foundation in fact, such as essential race superiority. It is obvious that their falsehood will be exposed upon investigation.

But exposing false ideas is not sufficient to remove prejudice. A prejudice (or predisposition or attitude) has an emotional content, and emotions react only very slowly to reason. A new emotional stimulus, such as that provided by religion, is required to prise the patient free from his prejudices.

New knowledge changes the intellectual picture, but the emotional change is slow to follow. When, however, the emotional change comes first, the intellectual change follows swiftly, often immediately. The reason for this is that man generally is quick to rationalize his emotional outlook. This is illustrated in the case of a prejudice which may be held against some person or group. When proved untenable intellectually, the emotional attitude changes only slowly, and sometimes not at all; but if the emotional prejudice is dissolved first, the intellectual prejudice is quickly recognized as mistaken or silly.

The abandonment of prejudices calls for nothing less than the relinquishing of the emotional attitudes aroused in us in childhood. Such a process is painful. Is it not said that whatever is impressed on a child under seven is engraved on stone? Only an utterly 'radiant acquiescence' with the principle of Oneness, and all that it implies, can free us from these gargoyles.

[handwritten: always² 6000]

'Abdu'l-Bahá writes on this subject: *[handwritten: Wars]*

'And among the teachings of Bahá'u'lláh is that religious, racial, political, economic, and patriotic prejudices destroy the edifice of humanity. As long as these prejudices prevail, the world of humanity will not have rest. For a period of six thousand years history informs us about the world of humanity. During these six thousand years (it) has not been free from war, strife, murder, and bloodthirstiness. In every period war has been waged in one country or another, and that war was due either to religious prejudice, racial prejudice, political prejudice or patriotic prejudice. It has, therefore, been ascertained and proved that all prejudices are destructive of the human edifice. As long as these prejudices persist, the struggle for existence must remain dominant, and bloodthirstiness and rapacity continue. Therefore, even as was the case in the past, the world of humanity cannot be saved from the darkness of nature, and cannot attain illumination, except through the abandonment of prejudices and the acquisition of the morals of the Kingdom.' [41]

Bahá'u'lláh exposes the false foundation of these prejudices, explains how they have been fostered, and substitutes universal truths for them. Modern scholarship can do as much, and does carry on the work. But who can change the emotional attitudes? Only the Messenger of God, who evokes in the heart such universal love that in all creation nothing is seen but 'the Face of God'.

Differences in human beings are a source of beauty and wealth to humanity. As 'Abdu'l-Bahá explains:

'Consider the flowers of a garden. Though differing in kind, colour, form, and shape, yet, inasmuch as they are refreshed by the waters of one spring, revived by the breath of one wind, invigorated by the rays of one sun, this diversity increaseth their charm and addeth unto their beauty. How unpleasing to the eye if all the flowers and plants, the leaves and blossoms, the fruit, the branches and the trees of that garden were all of the same shape and colour! Diversity of hues, form and shape enricheth and adorneth the garden, and heighteneth the effect thereof. In like manner, when divers shades of thought, temperament and character, are brought together under the power and influence of one central agency, the beauty and glory of human perfection will be revealed and made manifest. Naught but the celestial potency of the Word of God, which ruleth and transcendeth the realities of all things, is capable of harmonizing the divergent thoughts, sentiments, ideas and convictions of the children of men.' [42]

Prejudice consists not only in preconceived ideas, but in obstinate attachment to outworn beliefs, methods and institutions. Dogmatism and infatuation with our own theories impede the establishment of universal peace just as much as other prejudices.

Abandonment of prejudice, therefore, implies not

only a change in attitude, but a change in the social,
economic and political structure of the world. 'The
call of Bahá'u'lláh is primarily directed against all
forms of provincialism, all insularities and prejudices. If long-cherished ideals and time-honoured
institutions, if certain social assumptions and religious formulae have ceased to promote the welfare
of the generality of mankind, if they no longer
minister to the needs of a continually evolving
humanity, let them be swept away and relegated to
the limbo of obsolescent and forgotten doctrines.
Why should these, in a world subject to the im-
mutable law of change and decay, be exempt from
the deterioration that must needs overtake every
human institution? For legal standards, political
and economic theories are solely designed to safeguard the interests of humanity as a whole, and not
humanity to be crucified for the preservation of . . .
any particular law or doctrine.' [43]

4

Universal Education

The theory that education is bad for the masses
has mercifully disappeared, or almost so. But when
Bahá'u'lláh, a century ago, declared that every individual, boy and girl, must receive a sound education, he was encroaching upon the prerogative of
the aristocracy. In earlier days education had been
monopolized by the priests.

But in this new cycle no classes or sections of
society are to be more favoured than others; every

individual is of value to the community and must be capable of taking part in the administration of its affairs. 'Abdu'l-Bahá has likened education to gardening, showing how the natural, unrestrained wilderness, can be changed into ordered beauty. Education cannot change characters, which are all different, but it can assist them to develop to their utmost capacity.

'The Prophets also acknowledge this opinion, to wit: that education hath a great effect upon the human race, but they declare that minds and comprehensions are originally different. And this matter is self-evident; it cannot be refuted. We see that certain children of the same age, nativity, and race, nay from the same household, under the tutorship of one teacher, differ in their minds and comprehensions. . . . No matter how much the shell is polished, it can never become the radiant pearl. The black stone will not become the world illuming gem . . . That is to say, training doth not change the human entity, but it produceth a marvellous effect. By this effective power all that is registered, in latency, of virtues and capacities in the human reality will be revealed. . . . It is for this reason that, in this new cycle, education and training are recorded in the Book of God as obligatory and not voluntary.' [44]

Education is a most important subject and we might spend many hours discussing it, not only from the viewpoint of what is taught, but considering such powerful instruments as the press, films, radio and television. Such discussion, however, is best left to the educators. We simply record that Bahá'u'lláh makes education compulsory for all, and that character training, and preparation for a profession or trade, are essential parts of Bahá'í education.

5

Equality of Men and Women

Considering the time and place in which Bahá'u'lláh proclaimed his principles, this one was probably the most revolutionary and startling of them all. And yet it is now the most universally accepted— outwardly at least.

Feminine emancipation has swept the world, both West and East, and women have proved their capacity to enter the professions, trades and arts, on an equal footing with men. But this is only a superficial equality—concessions extorted from a 'man's world'.* Full psychic equality is not yet; men are unwilling to recognize it, and women, owing to thousands of years of inferior education and position, are unable to accept it.

There are many deep significances in this principle. 'Abdu'l-Bahá said:

'The world of humanity has two wings; one is woman and the other man. Not until both wings are equally developed can the bird fly. Should one

* Female labour is still cheaper than male.

wing remain weak, flight is impossible. Not until the world of woman becomes equal to the world of man in the acquisition of virtues and perfections, can success and prosperity be attained as they ought to be.'[45]

Men and women are not the same; they have different functions. But these functions are complementary and both must be equal for a perfect result.

In psychological terms we say there are two principles, Logos the male, and Eros the female. So far, Logos, the active, achieving principle has been dominant in world affairs. Eros, the principle which brings people into relatedness and maintains harmony, has been in the background or confined to the family. But its power and value is unconsciously recognized in the fact that the woman—the hostess—is the important person at a social gathering; the mother in the home.

When this force is released into all human affairs, it will accomplish its work between nations, in the human family.

The excesses to which women have been led by their sudden and swift emancipation—their attempts to achieve equality through sacrifice o femininity, or through outdoing men in masculine activities—offer no standard of judgment for a truly mature sex. Equality of women does not mean that they must make better males than men, but that they must achieve true maturity of soul. The same obligation rests upon men.

6

The Adoption of an International Auxiliary Language

'In all the world there is nothing more important than to be understood by your fellowmen, for upon this depends the progress of
civilization itself.'[46]

Since this principle was proclaimed by Bahá'u'l-
láh, Esperanto, Basic English and a number of other
world languages have been invented. Esperanto
has probably gained the most popular support, and
in nearly all European countries and in America
enthusiasts are to be found.

Speaking before the Esperanto Society in Edin-
burgh in 1913 'Abdu'l-Bahá said: 'I pray you,
Esperantists and non-Esperantists, to work with
zeal for the spread of this language, for it will
hasten the coming of that day, that millennial day,
foretold by prophets and seers . . .'[46]

On another occasion he said that one man could
not make the world language, but it would have to
be compiled by an international committee.

'Only think how the International Language
will facilitate intercommunication among all the
nations of the earth. Half of our lives are consumed in acquiring a knowledge of languages, for
in this enlightened age every man who hopes to
travel in Asia and Africa and Europe must learn
several languages, in order that he may converse
with their peoples. But no sooner does he
acquire one language than another is needed.

Thus one's whole life may be passed in acquiring those languages which are a hindrance to international communication. The International Language frees humanity from all these problems. . . .

'Oneness of language will transform mankind into one world, remove religious misunderstandings and unite East and West in the spirit of brotherhood and love. Oneness of language will change this world from many families into one family. This auxiliary international language will gather the nations under one standard, as if the five continents of the world had become one, for then mutual interchange of thought will be possible for all. It will remove ignorance and superstition, since each child of whatever race or nation can pursue his studies in science and art, needing but two languages—his own and the International. The world of matter will become the expression of the world of mind. Then discoveries will be revealed, inventions will multiply, the sciences advance by leaps and bounds, the scientific culture of the earth will develop along broader lines. Then the nations will be enabled to utilize the latest and best thought, because expressed in the International Language.' [46]

It is not intended that there should be only one language. The international tongue and script is to be auxiliary. National culture, literature, art, genius, are to be preserved and developed, but all people must learn at least two languages; their native tongue and the international tongue. Unity in diversity is the desired result, not uniformity, and it is to be hoped that the world language will be spoken with many a burr and accent.

7

Other principles of Bahá'u'lláh will each require separate chapters. Here is a list of the basic ones, which indicates the all-embracing nature of the Bahá'í Faith.

The Oneness of Mankind.

The Oneness of Religion.

An Unfettered Search after Truth.

The Abandonment of Prejudice and Superstition.

Universal Compulsory Education.

Equality of Men and Women.

Adoption of an International Auxiliary Language.

The Harmony of Religion and Science.

Economic Principles:

> work for all; abolition of extremes of poverty and wealth.

A World Legislature.

A World Tribunal.

Universal Peace.

It should not be assumed that the Bahá'í Faith is simply a system or code of ethics. There are mysteries, such as the nature of man, his soul, mind and spirit; the nature of the universe; the relationship of man to God; the mystery of creation; the purpose of life; immortality. Bahá'u'lláh's teachings on all these subjects are deep and enlightening, and given with the authority of a Manifestation of God.

This modern statement of religion is wholly satisfying to modern man 'in search of a soul'. It is, in truth, the 'water of life' gushing forth once more from the same spring. Who drinks of it is born again; who refuses it remains an intellectual embryo.

Through this rebirth, and through these principles which make for an ordered world, the whole of mankind may find salvation from the terrors of this age, and a doorway to a new and more splendid life.

CHAPTER V

RELIGION AND SCIENCE

THE conflict between religion and science is not new. History provides numberless examples of scientists who have been persecuted in the name of religion and forced with horrible tortures to deny their discoveries.

Lately, the pendulum has swung the other way, and religion now has to adapt its theological universe to the realities uncovered by science.

Bahá'u'lláh insists on the harmony of these two functions of the human spirit. Both are approaches to Truth, and cannot be in opposition. Scientists and parsons may disagree, and either may be wrong, but Science, which is knowledge of the universe, cannot be opposed to Religion, which is the art of living.

It is of no help at all to speak of materialism and idealism, for there are idealists and materialists in both camps.

The trouble arises from the fact that religionists, having built a universe based on the literal meaning of Scripture, fought, and do fight, tooth and nail against the inevitable collapse of such a system. See how geography was opposed because it taught that the earth was round, and therefore hell and heaven couldn't be 'down' and 'up'. Astronomy, which removed our planet from the most important position in the sky, biology and the other sciences which lent their weight to theories of evolution and placed the age of the earth much higher than the fundamentalist's six thousand years, all were opposed by the champions of man's universe, as against the discoverers of the Creator's.

Science is free of this rigidity. In fact, the chief characteristic of the scientific picture is its flexibility. Science never declares an ultimate; it is always willing to hear fresh information and evidence and to change its conclusions if necessary.

Religion, in the hands of organizations and doctrinaires, refuses to accept the progressiveness of revelation, from which it is derived (the Jews would not accept Christ nor the Christians Muḥammad), thereby causing its own incapacity to keep up to date. The Bible records four thousand years of progressive revelation up to the time of Christ, at which time, according to Christian creeds, revelation ceased. On the basis of this assumption the Churches offer to mankind, or part of it, the remnants of a once great system, and reject the new outpouring of spiritual Truth and vitality, promised in the Gospel.

Science does not oppose the moral precepts inculcated by religion, but it does occasionally recommend the adoption of new practices and the discontinuance of old ones, in order to promote the general welfare. But in general, science is confined to investigation and the production of facts, and it is up to the rest of humanity to make the best use of them. And it is here that religion plays its part: for upon the spiritual condition of mankind depend the uses to which scientific power is put, whether to the enrichment or the destruction of human life. The awful efficiency of death-dealing instruments, the poverty and want and misery of vast numbers of human beings, the rampant national and class hatreds, provide incontrovertible testimony to the hollowness of present-day religion.

If science opposes this kind of religion, so does every sane human being. For science subscribes immeasurably to the betterment of life. It relieves us of the most arduous and dangerous tasks and gives us the power of sufficient wealth to provide for everybody's needs. It offers us a healthier, longer life than our fathers enjoyed; it gives us the means of greatly minimizing, perhaps eliminating, deformity, insanity, and disease; it provides the means whereby the work of feeding, clothing, housing and organizing can be carried out more efficiently than ever before without requiring us to spend all our lifetime doing it; by finding other means of power than coal and oil, it enables us to do away with the grime and soot and smell of industry. It gives us the means of a civilized freedom. But we continue to blow each other to pieces, to burn each other's lungs, twist each other's bodies and deprive our fellows of the means of livelihood.

This is the failure of religion, not of science. 'Abdu'l-Bahá said in New York:

'Science cannot create amity and fellowship in human hearts. Neither can patriotism not racial allegiance effect a remedy. It must be accomplished solely through the divine bounties and spiritual bestowals which have descended from God in this day for that purpose. This is an exigency of the times and the divine remedy has been provided. The spiritual teachings of the religion of God can alone create this love, unity and accord in human hearts.'[47]

Religion, striving to maintain a rational idealism, censures science for its undiluted materialism. The late J. B. S. Haldane, in an article entitled 'Science, Morals and Religion' takes up the charge made by a leading divine, that Science bases all its structure of logic and reason on the sole principles of the 'unity and self-sufficiency of the material universe' and the capacity to be measured as the only valid proof of existence. He refutes this charge and says that the 'self-sufficiency of the material universe' is only 'a useful working hypothesis, useful above all because it can be tested' and he goes on to show that science regards 'certain theorems, such as the conservation of energy as a great deal more reliable than any law based on measurement'.

From this we may gather a very fair idea of the scientific attitude—an approach to truth by a process of investigation starting from an hypothesis which works and advancing on the structure of conclusions which have been severely tested and which must also work, a process which involves constant reinvestigation and modification of conclusions and which leaves no avenue of information unexplored. Several noted scientists have explained that the hypotheses and conclusions of science are no more than diagrams which fit the known facts, and inasmuch as known facts are constantly being supplemented the diagram is constantly changing. Eventually, of course, the original hypothesis itself may prove untenable, in which case science will have to find another one. And here is the real beauty of science; it will find another one, for science does not cling dogmatically to original conclusions which have been enlarged and amended.

But the overthrow of an axiom by no means proves the uselessness of discoveries based upon it. The conception of pressure of gases held many years ago may have been superseded but this does not alter the value of the parachute, and if scientists were to reach a point tomorrow where the self-sufficiency of the material universe no longer worked as a basis for investigation, the findings of biology and physics would still stand.

Science is not the invention of brilliant minds; it is based on reality in all its branches. Its mathematical calculations are the same as those of the universe. The inhabitants of the Milky Way, if there are any besides ourselves, would recognize a circle, and the value of it to them would be the same as to us, though they might not use the same symbol.

In view of the rational nature of science and the

dogmatic attitude of religion, reconciliation would seem to be impossible. But in any fair investigation we must distinguish between the present array of theological doctrine and the tremendous power of real religion which has so often been evidenced in history. Religion, purged of its cant and superstition and apathy, can again give spiritual life to mankind, and it would be more than foolish to turn away from it.

2

If man is to enjoy inward peace, science and religion must agree; reason and faith must be in full accord.

This will mean drastic modification of much of the teaching of the churches. Such modification has already been made to the symbolism of the Old Testament—as for instance the story of the Garden of Eden, but the symbolism of the New Testament is still taught in its literal meaning. For instance, the resurrection of Jesus, and the ascent of His body to 'heaven' are essential dogmas in a confession of Christian faith, in their literal meaning! How can this sort of religion be in harmony with science and reason, how can men have faith in this sort of thing? And to what end? Did Jesus come to conquer the death of the body—which the Creator has ordained, or to conquer spiritual death, which is the result of man's sin?

'Abdu'l-Bahá explains that religious truth is revealed to man according to the capacity of the age, and the language in which it has been expressed has been suited to the same end. Thus Moses' categorical imperatives: 'Thou shalt . . .'; 'Thou shalt not . . .' Jesus spoke in parables. Bahá'u'lláh speaks of atoms, of biology, evolutions, electrons, and other suns behind our own. Each revelation is a perfect expression of 'the spirit of the age'.

The Bahá'í attitude to science is set forth by 'Abdu'l-Bahá in a talk given in Washington, D.C., on April 23rd, 1912, from which we quote:

'The virtues of humanity are many but science is the most noble of them all. The distinction which man enjoys above and beyond the station of the animal is due to this paramount virtue. It is a bestowal of God; it is not material, it is divine. Science is an effulgence of the Sun of Reality, the power of investigating and discovering the verities of the universe, the means by which man finds a pathway to God. All the powers and attributes of man are human and hereditary in origin, outcomes of nature's processes, except the intellect, which is supernatural. Through intellectual and intelligent inquiry science is the discoverer of all things. It unites present and past, reveals the history of bygone nations and events, and confers upon man today the essence of all human knowledge and attainment throughout the ages. By intellectual processes and logical deductions of reason, this super power in man can penetrate the mysteries of the future and anticipate its happenings.

'Science is the first emanation from God toward man. All created beings embody the potentiality of material perfection, but the power of intellectual investigation and scientific acquisition is a higher virtue specialized to man alone. Other beings and organisms are deprived of this potentiality and attainment. God has created or deposited this love of reality in man. The development and progress of a nation is according to the measure and degree of that nation's scientific attainments. Through this means, its greatness is continually increased and day by day the welfare and prosperity of its people are assured.'[48]

Nevertheless,

'Man has two powers, and his development two aspects. One power is connected with the material world and by it he is capable of material advancement. The other power is spiritual and through its development his inner, potential nature is awakened. These powers are like two wings. Both must be developed, for flight is impossible with one wing. Praise be to God! material advancement has been evident in the world but there is need of spiritual advancement in like proportion. We must strive unceasingly and without rest to accomplish the development of the spiritual nature in man, and endeavor with tireless energy to advance humanity towards the nobility of its true and intended station.'[49]

'Otherwise, by simple development along material lines man is not perfected. At most, the physical aspect of man, his natural or material conditions may become stabilized and improved

the order of appearance of life was first sea vegetables, then fishes, then amphibians, then reptiles, then birds, then mammals and finally, man? This is the same order as mineral, vegetable, animal and man.

'Abdu'l-Bahá states that although man was once in the different vegetable and animal forms, he was always a distinct species. Although he once hung by his tail he was potentially man, and not a monkey. Thus through the thousands of years that man has existed on earth monkeys or other vertebrates have not been imbued with the spirit of man and have not been able to discover radio or the atomic theory, or to overcome in the slightest the limitations of the natural world.

Bahá'u'lláh in the Hidden Words reveals:

'O Son of Bounty! Out of the wastes of nothingness, with the clay of My command I made thee to appear, and have ordained for thy training every atom in existence and the essence of all created things. Thus, ere thou didst issue from thy mother's womb, I destined for thee two founts of gleaming milk, eyes to watch over thee, and hearts to love thee. Out of My loving-kindness, 'neath the shade of My mercy I nurtured thee, and guarded thee by the essence of My grace and favour. And My purpose in all this was that thou mightest attain My everlasting dominion and become worthy of My invisible bestowals. And yet heedless thou didst remain, and when fully grown, thou didst neglect all My bounties and occupied thyself with thine idle imaginings, in such wise that thou didst become wholly forgetful, and, turning away from the portals of the Friend didst abide within the courts of My enemy.' [51]

Such is the Bahá'í teaching on the subject of emergent evolution. Do not religion and science agree?

*   *   *

With regard to the perfect order which is found throughout the universe, from a blade of grass to the spiral nebulae, 'Abdu'l-Bahá says:

'Love is the highest law in this great universe of God. Love is the law of order between simple essences, whereby they are apportioned and united into compound substances in this world of matter. Love is the essential and magnetic power that organizes the planets and the stars which shine in infinite space. Love supplies the impulse to that intense and unceasing meditation which reveals the hidden mysteries of the universe.'

4

Atoms, attracted through 'elective affinity', form simple elements and these elements in turn compose to form phenomena. Hence the existence of forms depends upon composition and their non-existence upon disintegration. Then where is the need for a Creator?

'Abdu'l-Bahá answers this in the following manner:

There are only three ways in which elements can compose. Accidentally, Involuntarily, and Voluntarily.

Composition cannot be accidental for in this case we should have an effect without a cause. If it is involuntary then there must be an inherent property in the elements which would force them to compose and in this case they would not be able to decompose. But all forms do decompose; therefore, composition cannot be involuntary. It follows that it must be voluntary, or through an act of will. That will is the Creative Will, or Will of God, executed by spirit.

'This is a rational proof, that the Will of the Creator is effected through the process of composition.' ('Abdu'l-Bahá.)

*   *   *

It seems likely, from scientific evidence, that a day will come when life can no longer exist on this planet, for the sun, according to astronomers, is annihilating itself at a tremendous rate. This is nowhere denied in the Bahá'í teachings, but that creation can come to an end is emphatically refuted. 'Abdu'l-Bahá says:

'The world of creation has had no beginning and will have no end, because it is the arena upon which the attributes and qualities of the spirit are being manifested. Can we limit God and His power? In the same manner we cannot limit His creations and attributes. Just as the reality of divinity is limitless likewise His grace and bounties are limitless.'

'Gaze upward through immeasurable space to the majestic order of the colossal suns. These luminous bodies are numberless. Behind our solar system there are unfathomable stellar systems; above these, are the remote aggregations of the milky way. Extend your vision beyond the fixed stars and again you shall behold many spheres of light. Indeed, the creation of the Almighty is beyond the grasp of the human intellect.'

5

It would be wearisome to dwell at length upon the scientific statements to be found in the Bahá'í teachings—they would fill a volume. Rather, we wish to show that there is no conflict between science and true religion.

In numberless passages Bahá'u'lláh and 'Abdu'l-Bahá have referred to the importance and high station of knowledge, and have commanded not only that knowledge must not be suppressed but that every impulse must be given to its dissemination. There is nothing which must be banned or blacklisted.

But knowledge and scientific invention are not, in themselves, capable of making an ordered world. We have both today in an unprecedented degree,

but spiritually we are incapable of making constructive use of these great powers. Therefore, man
must be spiritually awakened before we can hope
for world peace or world order. And this is the
mission of Bahá'u'lláh. This is the mission of all
the Prophets: the education of the spirit of man, so
that it will continue to acquire higher and higher
virtues and be the cause of love and harmony which
are the guiding principles of the universe.

CHAPTER VI

WORLD COMMONWEALTH

MANY utopias and schemes for a new world order have been offered to twentieth-century man. Most of them fail to emphasize or even to acknowledge the fact, that social order rests upon individual conduct. Hard work, independence, good character, self-discipline, are the foundations of civilization. It cannot be imposed from the top according to somebody's blue-print. The disastrous attempts in the twentieth century make this only too clear.

The Bahá'í Faith does not offer something for nothing—peace, prosperity, culture and leisure without the price, *in advance*, of spiritual and intellectual striving. These things are possible today, but they have to be won.

The world order of Bahá'u'lláh is a goal which we can visualize in outline, and towards which we may strive. It is no magic millennium which will result from some particular political or economic action. It is founded on the spiritual concept of the oneness of mankind and raises a structure by which this unity may be preserved and developed. '*The earth is but one country, and mankind its citizens*' is its principle.[52]

A world state, founded on such a principle, cannot tolerate the existence of dominant and subservient peoples; it cannot permit the exploitation of backward members of the human family by more advanced ones; it cannot recognize the right of any part of that family to make war on another part, or even to maintain armaments; it cannot allow any part of that commonwealth to monopolize raw materials, which are needed by all members; it cannot accept the poverty of the great majority of its citizens when by their industry and the aid of science, they can produce plenty for all.

The control of these matters is not possible as long as nations recognize no higher authority than themselves. The outlaw is one who refuses to cede his personal sovereignty to the law of society. The nations of the world—all of them—have committed the same crime with respect to the society of mankind. They refuse to cede their sovereignty to the demands of international law and order.

The world commonwealth envisioned by Bahá'u'lláh is governed by a world authority, that is, a World Legislature freely elected by the peoples of the earth. It must have authority to enforce its decisions upon any dilatory or rebellious member of the commonwealth, and such action must be as swift and certain as it would be in the case of an individual who breaks the law. No such world government can succeed unless backed by the authority of the whole human race, which brings us again to the principles of oneness and complete

D

abandonment of prejudice, on which the future of mankind depends.

Bahá'u'lláh, in his *Tablet to Queen Victoria*, addresses the 'concourse of the rulers of the earth':

'Take ye counsel together, and let your concern be only for that which profiteth mankind and bettereth the condition thereof. . . . Regard the world as the human body which, though created whole and perfect, has been afflicted, through divers causes, with grave ills and maladies. Not for one day did it rest, nay its sicknesses waxed more severe, as it fell under the treatment of unskilled physicians who have spurred on the steed of their worldly desires and have erred grievously. And if at one time, through the care of an able physician, a member of that body was healed, the rest remained afflicted as before. Thus informeth you the All-Knowing, the All-Wise. . . . That which the Lord hath ordained as the sovereign remedy and the mightiest instrument for the healing of all the world is the union of all its peoples in one universal Cause, one common Faith. This can in no wise be achieved except through the power of a skilled, an all-powerful and inspired Physician. This verily is the truth, and all else naught but error.' [53]

In a further passage he adds:

'We see you adding every year unto your expenditures and laying the burden thereof on the people whom ye rule; this verily is naught but grievous injustice. Fear the sighs and tears of this Wronged One, and burden not your peoples

beyond that which they can endure. . . . Be reconciled among yourselves, that ye may need
armaments no more save in a measure to safeguard your territories and dominions. Be united,
O concourse of the sovereigns of the world, for
thereby will the tempest of discord be stilled
amongst you and your peoples find rest. Should
any one among you take up arms against another,
rise ye all against him, for this is naught but
manifest justice.' [54]

It is explained by 'Abdu'l-Bahá that '*in a measure to
safeguard your territories and dominions*' means internal
police only. All international policing is to be done
by the world government.

In this World State, the less developed countries
will be under the direct protection of the world
government. Their rights as individual members
of the world commonwealth will be preserved and
upheld. They will be assisted, when necessary, by
the employment of experts—chemists, engineers,
administrators, etc., and world resources will be
available for their development.

This world authority must, in the interests of the
whole human race, establish law in the place of war;
it must strictly limit the armed forces of every
nation, according to their internal needs. It must
plan and put into practice a world system of economics which will remove the present evils of
waste, inferior quality, want in the midst of plenty.
It must assume sole control over tariffs, excise,
sources of raw material. It must establish a world

currency and a world bank, and select an international language to be taught in the schools together with the native tongue. It must foster a spirit of world citizenship among all the peoples of the planet.

In addition to the world legislative body, there is needed a world court, a Supreme Tribunal whose decisions shall be binding on all parties. This will replace the arbitrament of war.

'Abdu'l-Bahá wrote, in *The Secret of Divine Civilization*:

'True civilization will unfurl its banner in the midmost heart of the world whenever a certain number of its distinguished and high-minded sovereigns—the shining exemplars of devotion and determination—shall, for the good and happiness of all mankind, arise, with firm resolve and clear vision, to establish the Cause of Universal Peace. They must make the Cause of Peace the object of general consultation, and seek by every means in their power to establish a Union of the nations of the world. They must conclude a binding treaty and establish a covenant, the provisions of which shall be sound, inviolable and definite. They must proclaim it to all the world and obtain for it the sanction of all the human race. This supreme and noble undertaking—the real source of the peace and well-being of all the world—should be regarded as sacred by all that dwell on earth. All the forces of humanity must be mobilized to ensure the stability and permanence of this Most Great

Covenant. In this all-embracing Pact the limits and frontiers of each and every nation should be clearly fixed, the principles underlying the relations of governments towards one another definitely laid down, and all international agreements and obligations ascertained. In like manner, the size of the armaments of every government should be strictly limited, for if the preparations for war and the military forces of any nation should be allowed to increase, they will arouse the suspicion of others. The fundamental principle underlying this solemn Pact should be so fixed that if any government later violate any of its provisions, all the governments on earth should arise to reduce it to utter submission, nay the human race as a whole should resolve, with every power at its disposal, to destroy that government. Should this greatest of all remedies be applied to the sick body of the world, it will assuredly recover from its ills and will remain eternally safe and secure.' [55]

This Covenant differs from the covenant of the League of Nations or the Charter of the United Nations, for both bodies have proved powerless in the face of interested opposition. In a *Letter to the Central Organization for a Durable Peace, The Hague*, written in 1919, we find:

'. . . although the League of Nations has been brought into existence, yet it is incapable of establishing Universal Peace. But the Supreme Tribunal which . . . Bahá'u'lláh has described will fulfil this sacred task with the utmost might and power. And His plan is this: that the national assemblies of each country and nation—that is to say parliaments—should elect two or three persons who are the choicest men of that nation, and are well informed concerning international laws and the relations between governments and aware of the essential needs of the world of humanity in this day. The number of these representatives should be in proportion to the number of inhabitants of that country. The election of these souls who are chosen by the national assembly, that is, the parliament, must be confirmed by the upper house, the congress and the cabinet and also by the president or monarch so these persons may be the elected ones of all the nation and the government. From among these people the members of the Supreme Tribunal will be elected, and all mankind will thus have a share therein, for every one of these delegates is fully representative of his nation. When the Supreme Tribunal gives a ruling on any international question, whether unanimously or by majority rule, there will no longer be any pretext for the plaintiff or ground of objection for the defendant. In case any of the governments or nations, in the execution of the irrefutable decision of the Supreme Tribunal, be negligent or dilatory, the rest of the nations will rise up against it,* because all the governments and nations of the world are the supporters of this Supreme Tribunal. Consider what a firm foundation this is. But by a limited and restricted League the purpose will

* Not in a world war, but by means of a World Executive.

not be realized as it ought and should. This is the truth about the situation which has been stated.'[56]

That most modern of men, Harry Emerson Fosdick, has said that 'Peace is not something we fall into because we react against war. Peace is a positive achievement involving an organized world community of law and order which we must want so much that we are willing to pay the full price it costs.'

That full price is the relinquishing of our cherished prejudices; it means the sacrifice of selfish ambitions, the daily striving to practise the Divine Art of Living, and the recognition of the oneness of humanity. Above all it means the relinquishing of uncurbed national sovereignty. The right to make and wage war, which each nation claims as its inalienable right, must be ceded to the demands of a world state. Punishment of a recalcitrant government must be as swift and sure as punishment of an individual who starts to break shop windows. The nature of the tribunal, already described, ensures its impartiality.

Commenting on a passage in Bahá'u'lláh's letter to Queen Victoria, Shoghi Effendi says, 'What else could these weighty words signify if they did not point to the inevitable curtailment of unfettered national sovereignty as an indispensable preliminary to the formation of the future Commonwealth of all the nations of the world? Some form of a world Super-State must needs be evolved, in

whose favour all the nations of the world will have
willingly ceded every claim to make war, certain
rights to impose taxation and all rights to maintain
armaments, except for purposes of maintaining
internal order within their respective dominions.
Such a state will have to include within its orbit an
International Executive adequate to enforce supreme and unchallengeable authority on every
recalcitrant member of the commonwealth; a
World Parliament whose members shall be elected
by the people in their respective countries and
whose election shall be confirmed by their respective
governments; and a Supreme Tribunal whose
judgment will have a binding effect even in such
cases where the parties concerned did not voluntarily agree to submit their case to its consideration.
A world community in which all economic barriers
will have been permanently demolished and the
interdependence of Capital and Labour definitely
recognized; in which the clamour of religious
fanaticism and strife will have been forever stilled;
in which the flame of racial animosity will have been
finally extinguished; in which a single code of
international law—the product of the considered
judgment of the world's federated representatives—
shall have as its sanction the instant and coercive
intervention of the combined forces of the federated
units; and finally a world community in which the
fury of a capricious and militant nationalism will
have been transmuted into an abiding consciousness
of world citizenship—such indeed, appears, in its

broadest outline, the Order anticipated by Bahá'u'l-láh, an Order that shall come to be regarded as the fairest fruit of a slowly maturing age.' [57]

This new age, this new cycle of human power, revolves around a new principle, the principle of Unity. 'Unification of the whole of mankind is the hall-mark of the stage which human society is now approaching. Unity of family, of tribe, of city-state, and nation have been successively attempted and fully established. World unity is the goal towards which a harassed humanity is striving. Nation-building has come to an end. The anarchy inherent in state sovereignty is moving towards a climax. A world, growing to maturity, must abandon this fetish, recognize the oneness and wholeness of human relationships, and establish once for all the machinery that can best incarnate this fundamental principle of its life.' [58]

'"A new life," Bahá'u'lláh proclaims, "is, in this age, stirring within all the peoples of the earth; and yet none hath discovered its cause, or perceived its motive." "O ye children of men," He thus addresses His generation, "the fundamental purpose animating the Faith of God and His Religion is to safeguard the interests and promote the unity of the human race . . . This is the straight path, the fixed and immovable foundation. Whatsoever is raised on this foundation, the changes and chances of the world can never impair its strength, nor will the revolution of countless centuries undermine its structure."

"The well-being of mankind," He declares, "its peace and security are unattainable unless and until its unity is firmly established." "So powerful is the light of unity," is His further testimony, "that it can illuminate the whole earth. The one true God, He Who knoweth all things, Himself testifieth to the truth of these words . . . This goal excelleth every other goal, and this aspiration is the monarch of all aspirations." "He Who is your Lord, the All-Merciful," He, moreover, has written, "cherisheth in His heart the desire of beholding the entire human race as one soul and one body. Haste ye to win your share of God's good grace and mercy in this Day that eclipseth all other created days." '[59]

'The unity of the human race, as envisaged by Bahá'u'lláh, implies the establishment of a world commonwealth in which all nations, races, creeds and classes are closely and permanently united, and in which the autonomy of its state members and the personal freedom and initiative of the individuals that compose them are definitely and completely safeguarded. This commonwealth must, as far as we can visualize it, consist of a world legislature, whose members will, as the trustees of the whole of mankind, ultimately control the entire resources of all the component nations, and will enact such laws as shall be required to regulate the life, satisfy the needs and adjust the relationships of all races and peoples. A world executive, backed by an international Force, will carry out the decisions arrived

at, and apply the laws enacted by, this world
legislature, and will safeguard the organic unity of
the whole commonwealth. A world tribunal will
adjudicate and deliver its compulsory and final
verdict in all and any disputes that may arise between
the various elements constituting this universal
system. A mechanism of world inter-communica-
tion will be devised, embracing the whole planet,
freed from national hindrances and restrictions, and
functioning with marvellous swiftness and perfect
regularity. A world metropolis will act as the nerve
centre of a world civilization, the focus towards
which the unifying forces of life will converge and
from which its energizing influences will radiate. A
world language will either be invented or chosen
from among the existing languages and will be
taught in the schools of all the federated nations as
an auxiliary to their mother tongue. A world script,
a world literature, a uniform and universal system of
currency, of weights and measures, will simplify and
facilitate intercourse and understanding among the
nations and races of mankind. In such a world
society, science and religion, the two most potent
forces in human life, will be reconciled, will co-
operate, and will harmoniously develop. The press
will, under such a system, while giving full scope to
the expression of the diversified views and convictions of mankind, cease to be mischievously
manipulated by vested interests, whether private or
public, and will be liberated from the influence of
contending governments and peoples. The eco-

nomic resources of the world will be organized, its sources of raw materials will be tapped and fully utilized, its markets will be co-ordinated and developed, and the distribution of its products will be equitably regulated.

'National rivalries, hatreds, and intrigues will cease, and racial animosity and prejudice will be replaced by racial amity, understanding and co-operation. The causes of religious strife will be permanently removed, economic barriers and restrictions will be completely abolished, and the inordinate distinction between classes will be obliterated. Destitution on the one hand, and gross accumulation of ownership on the other, will disappear. The enormous energy dissipated and wasted on war, whether economic or political, will be consecrated to such ends as will extend the range of human inventions and technical development, to the increase of the productivity of mankind, to the extermination of disease, to the extension of scientific research, to the raising of the standard of physical health, to the sharpening and refinement of the human brain, to the exploitation of the unused and unsuspected resources of the planet, to the prolongation of human life, and to the furtherance of any other agency that can stimulate the intellectual, the moral, and spiritual life of the entire human race.

'A world federal system, ruling the whole earth and exercising unchallengeable authority over its unimaginably vast resources, blending and embodying the ideals of both the East and the West, liberated from the curse of war and its miseries, and bent on the exploitation of all the available sources of energy on the surface of the planet, a system in which Force is made the servant of Justice, whose life is sustained by its universal recognition of one God and by its allegiance to one common Revelation—such is the goal towards which humanity, impelled by the unifying forces of life, is moving.'* [60]

* Shoghi Effendi in *The Unfoldment of World Civilization.*

CHAPTER VII

SOCIAL ECONOMY

Bahá'u'lláh gives no cut and dried system of economics. He establishes certain basic principles and leaves it to us to build the structure.

There is a danger of the popular term 'new world order' conjuring up a picture of something for nothing; state-supported individuals enjoying all the advantages of prosperity without any adequate contribution of hard work or service.

Bahá'u'lláh requires everyone to work; no idle rich and no idle poor.

'The most despised of men before God is he who sits and begs,'[61] and 'The best of men are they that earn a livelihood by their calling and spend upon themselves and upon their kindred for the love of God, the Lord of all worlds.'[62]

Thus in spite of the fact that 'laissez faire' and unrestricted competition give way to socialization and co-operation, the basis of prosperity is still individual effort, hard work and independence.

'. . . it is incumbent on every one to engage in crafts and professions, for therein lies the secret of wealth, O men of understanding! . . . Trees that yield no fruit . . . will ever be for the fire.' [63]

2

The tragic absurdities of the twentieth century may well seem unbelievable to people of the future. Farmers are heavily subsidized not to produce food while the majority of the human race is in need. Huge sums are spent on public health while the water and air of the planet is constantly polluted. Deserts are created where none existed, species are exterminated and a 'silent spring' truly exists in large tracts of the countryside.

Governments spend great sums and efforts to achieve peace between active belligerents while simultaneously supplying both sides with arms. Posterity must be for ever amazed at a generation which could capture a beam from Arcturus to light the opening of a World's Fair, could land men on the moon, climb Everest, and yet tolerate the poverty and misery of millions in the midst of an overwhelming plenty, a generation which spends a vast proportion of its wealth on war.

Striking at the root of the problem, 'Abdu'l-Bahá says: '*The fundamentals of the whole economic condition are divine in nature and are associated with the world of the heart and spirit.*' [64] Speaking to a gathering of Socialists at Montreal in 1912, he said:

'Although the body politic is one family, yet because of lack of harmonious relations some members are comfortable and some in direst misery, some members are satisfied and some are hungry, some members are clothed in most costly garments and some families are in need of food and shelter. Why? Because this family (of mankind) lacks the necessary reciprocity and symmetry. This household is not well arranged. This household is not living under a perfect law. All the laws which are legislated do not insure happiness. They do not provide comfort. Therefore a law must be given to this family by means of which all the members of this family will enjoy equal well-being and happiness.' [65]

'Reciprocity and symmetry' ... these are the needs of the new social order. Co-operation must replace unbridled competition and an economic programme embracing the entire planet must be developed. This is the real economic problem, that in an age when co-operation is needed in human affairs, principles which served mankind success-fully during the age of competition, are still upheld and regarded as inviolate. They are lamentably effete as shown by results.

Tariffs, currency manipulation, monopoly of raw materials, low wages—these are the great sabo-teurs of world prosperity. But they are only agents —the real gangster is economic self-sufficiency. Nearly every nation, or group of nations, has tried to practise this, and has gloried in what it believed to be its ability to be self-supporting. At the same time every effort has been made to keep up 'foreign' trade, that is to sell the other man something with-out buying anything in return.

Economic self-sufficiency is born of fear and selfishness and leads straight to war. In this modern world all people are in need of each other, can supply each other's wants, and by the reciprocal action of buying and selling, contribute to an increasing standard of living—provided of course that the results of labour are equitably shared, and not concentrated in the hands of a minority. And the basis of equity must be universal, otherwise some nations will undersell all the others by using cheaper labour, and that will start the same old round again of tariffs, etc.

The economic problem, like every major difficulty facing us today, is insoluble except on a world scale. We cannot have poverty in one country and prosperity in the rest. Neither can we cure poverty and unemployment in one country alone; for nations are now, whether willingly or not, economically interdependent.

A World Legislature, such as that described in the previous chapter, can solve it. It can remove the barriers to international trade which result from the attempts of nations to be self-sufficient. It can liberate the energies now devoted to war for service to the arts of peace, and it can provide the necessary machinery for an easier and greater interchange of goods and services. Such things as a world currency, a world bank, a single system of weights and measures come within its charter. It must maintain free access to the raw materials of the planet, and protect the rights of all peoples; maintain a universal

E

minimum standard of living, and limit the economic power of individuals.

3

The social principle of Bahá'u'lláh is explained by 'Abdu'l-Bahá: '*First and foremost is the principle that to all the members of the body politic shall be given the greatest achievements of the world of humanity. Each one shall have the utmost welfare and well-being.*'[66] Although there are degrees in the social order, the minimum standard of living is the '*greatest achievements of the world of humanity*'.

> 'God is not partial and is no respecter of persons. He has made provision for all. The harvest comes forth for everyone. The rain showers upon everybody and the heat of the sun is destined to warm everyone . . . Therefore there should be for all humanity the utmost happiness, the utmost comfort, the utmost well-being.'[67]

Capital and Labour

'Abdu'l-Bahá explained, on more than one occasion, that the relationship between capital and labour could never be harmonized by strikes for higher wages. The governments of the world collectively, acting through the World Legislature, have the right to interfere and settle the problem. They should plan

> 'with utmost wisdom and power, so that neither the capitalists suffer from enormous losses, nor the labourers become needy. In the

utmost moderation they should make the law, then announce to the public that the rights of the working people are to be strongly preserved. Also the rights of the capitalists are to be protected. When such a general plan is adopted by the will of both sides, should a strike occur, all the governments of the world should resist it. Otherwise, the work will lead to much destruction, especially in Europe. Terrible things will take place. One of the several causes of a universal European war will be this question. For instance, the owners of properties, mines and factories should share their incomes with their employees, and give a certain fair percentage of their products to their working men, in order that the employees may receive, besides their wages, some of the general income of the factory, so that the employee may strive with his soul in the work.' [68]

'Then rules and laws should be established to regulate the excessive fortunes of certain private individuals, and limit the misery of millions of the poor masses; thus a certain moderation would be obtained. However, absolute equality is just as impossible, for absolute equality in fortunes, honours, commerce, agriculture, industry would end in a want of comfort, in discouragement, in disorganization of the means of existence, and in universal disappointment; the order of the community would be quite destroyed. Thus, there is a great wisdom in the fact that equality is not imposed by law; it is, therefore, preferable for moderation to do its work. The main point is, by means of laws and regulations to hinder the constitution of the excessive fortunes of certain individuals, and to protect the essential needs of the masses. . . . Therefore, laws and regulations should be established which would permit the workmen to receive from the factory owner their wages and a share in the fourth or the fifth part of the profits,* according to the capacity of the factory; or in some other way the body of workmen and the manufacturers should share equitably the profits and advantages. Indeed, the direction and administration of affairs come from the owner of the factory, and the work and labour, from the body of the workmen. In other words, the workmen should receive wages which ensure them an adequate support, and when they cease work, becoming feeble or helpless, they should receive from the owner of the factory a sufficient pension. The wages should be high enough to satisfy the workmen with the amount they receive, so that they may be able to put a little aside for days of want and helplessness.' [69]

'According to the Divine Law, employees should not be paid merely by wages. Nay, rather, they should be partners in every work.'

Disputes between capital and labour can be settled without violence when industry is built on this co-operative basis,

'But the mutual rights of both associated parties will be fixed and established according to custom by just and impartial laws. In case one of the two

* 'Abdu'l-Bahá emphasized that these figures were only an example, for illustration only.

parties should transgress, the courts of justice
would have to give judgment, and by an effica-
cious fine put an end to the transgression; thus
order will be re-established, and the difficulties
settled. The interference of courts of justice and
of the Government in difficulties pending between manufacturers and workmen is legal, for
the reason that current affairs between workmen
and manufacturers cannot be compared with
ordinary affairs between private persons, which
do not concern the public, and with which the
Government should not occupy itself. In reality,
although they appear to be matters between
private persons, these difficulties between patrons
and workmen produce a general detriment; for
commerce, industry, agriculture, and the general
affairs of the country are all intimately linked
together. If one of these suffers an abuse, the
detriment affects the mass. Thus the difficulties
between workmen and manufacturers become a
cause of general detriment.'[70]

4

In order to hinder the amassing of huge private
fortunes, Bahá'u'lláh recommends the division of
one's estate at death, among seven classes of heirs: off-
spring; wife; father; mother; brother; sister; teachers.

'Abdu'l-Bahá explained that this method of willing property is not compulsory, but is an abrogation
of the law of entail.

'In accordance with Bahá'u'lláh's teachings, a
Bahá'í can give all his property to his eldest son.

He may do just as he likes. As long as it is his own property he may do as he wishes. One's property cannot be snatched by another. There is one difference, however; when a Bahá'í leaves all to his eldest son, the eldest son in turn may break the line and divide as he wants to—according to Bahá'u'lláh's method, or as he wishes.'

5

In summarizing this chapter it must be emphasized that the Bahá'í teachings do not contain any detailed system of economics. The general plan is indicated but any great improvement in either social or economic conditions cannot be made until the spiritual condition is remedied. Humanity will revive and its affairs will prosper when it becomes conscious that a new day has dawned and when it is willing to let up the blinds and allow the sunlight to stream through its musty household.

Industry, crafts, and professions must no longer be regarded as fields of grim struggle; the individual is not an isolated unit battling for survival in a jungle of human greeds. Nor are there to be idle rich or idle poor. Work is service and worship. All must work.

A world economic system must be planned, capable of supplying the greatest achievements of humanity to everyone, a system in which reciprocity and symmetry replace the present disorderly competition.

The interdependence of capital and labour must

be fully recognized and industry must be placed on a co-operative basis, so that the mutual interests of both sides are promoted. When this is done by agreement the courts of justice will have the right to settle disputes.

Degrees of wealth and occupation are desirable but excessive fortunes are to be limited by taxation and the invalidating of the law of entail. Destitution is to be removed. Public revenue should be raised through a graduated system of taxation, such as most modern states have developed. An interesting feature of the Bahá'í proposal is the inclusion of 'voluntary donations' among the sources. This is perhaps the place to mention that the Bahá'í world community finances its activities entirely and solely through the voluntary contributions of recognized believers.

A minimum standard of living must be maintained and a graduated scale of income tax enforced. Those who have most will contribute most. All helpless and infirm people must be maintained in comfort by the state.

These are some of the outstanding features of the economics of the new world order. But the success of all human enterprise depends upon spiritual qualities. Justice, love, and the spirit of service are the foundation of true prosperity and peace.

Bahá'u'lláh, in common with all the Prophets, urges man to be detached from wealth and to turn his thoughts towards higher things but this does not mean giving up one's vocation. Indeed, *'it is*

incumbent on every one to engage in crafts and profes-
sions . . .' [71] and such action is, he says, *'identical with*
the worship of God . . .' [72]

'All humanity must obtain a livelihood by
sweat of the brow and bodily exertion; at the
same time seeking to lift the burden of others,
striving to be the source of comfort to souls, and
facilitating the means of living. This in itself is
devotion to God. But the energies of the heart
must not be completely occupied with them.
Though the mind is busy the heart must be
attracted toward the Kingdom of God in order
that the virtues of humanity may be attained from
every direction and source.' [73]

Bahá'u'lláh commends the possession of wealth
if it is used well. In the *Tablet of Tarázát* he writes:

'. . . man should know his own self, and know
those things which lead to loftiness or to base-
ness, to shame or to honour, to affluence or to
poverty. After man has realized his own being
and become mature, then for him wealth [or com-
petence] is needed. If this wealth is acquired
through a craft and profession, it is approvable
and worthy of praise to men of wisdom, especially
to those servants who arise to train the world and
beautify the souls of nations.' [74]

The foundation of prosperity and social order is
none other than the spiritual commandment of
Jesus Christ, that you love your neighbour as yourself. Bahá'u'lláh shows us the practical application
of this command in the modern world.

CHAPTER VIII

ADMINISTRATION

RELIGION, for reasons which are indicated in Chapter V, has become divorced from other human activities. In fact, our dreadful western civilization has succeeded in dividing life (and therefore people) into separate compartments. Business, recreation, politics, religion, social life, are regarded as separate and distinct activities, to be assumed according to the time or day.

Religion should be the co-ordinator of all man's functions, the pervading spirit which gives meaning and purpose to his every action. This it is to Bahá'ís. The unique feature of the Bahá'í Administrative Order lies in the fact that it provides, not an ecclesiastical system, but a social channel through which the energy of a reborn humanity may find expression, and in which the spiritual principles of Bahá'u'lláh may vitalize all the varied aspects of life.

The standard example of the division between church and state is found in Christendom, where the saying of Jesus, '*Render to Caesar the things that are Caesar's, and to God the things that are God's,*'[75] was used, during the early bickerings between Pope and Emperor, as authority for investing temporal power in the Emperor and spiritual power in the

Pope. It actually worked out that the Pope, being on the spot,* and able, and generally willing, to conciliate the invader, exercised most of the power. Finally, however, when Leo III gave the crown of the Holy Roman Empire to Charlemagne, the schism was officially recognized. It was a blow from which Christendom has never recovered.

This separation of church and state, of government and religion, means that there are two standards of conduct . . . private and public, a condition tragically apparent in the present century when murder, arson, and robbery are condemned in the private citizen and indulged in and fiercely upheld as the prerogative of states.

In the World Order of Bahá'u'lláh there is no cleavage between religion and other human activities, whether they be governmental, economic or cultural. There is no professional priesthood and no professional politics, neither can economic power be wielded overwhelmingly by a minority, so that vested interests become translated into interests in the common good. Religion becomes the art of living and, through the Covenant of Bahá'u'lláh, the true source of unity.

The Covenant

In all previous religious systems the withdrawal of the Founder has left the way open for discord and party leadership. 'I am of Peter; I am of Paul', has been a characteristic of religion from the earliest

* The Emperor lived in Constantinople, the Pope in Rome.

revelations to the time of Islám, when the verbal appointment of 'Alí as successor was disputed and a division made. We have only to call to mind the existing faiths to realize that they are all divided into numerous sects.

There are no Bahá'í sects. There never can be.

The Bahá'í Dispensation is protected from schism by the unique station of 'Abdu'l-Bahá, clearly stated in Bahá'u'lláh's Will. Upon him Bahá'u'lláh conferred the station of Centre of His Covenant and made him the sole interpreter of the Teachings. His word is equal in validity, though subordinate in rank, to Bahá'u'lláh's own. As a consequence of this, the vicious attacks which were made upon the Faith after the ascension of Bahá'u'lláh, were powerless to impair its unity.

'Abdu'l-Bahá perpetuated the Covenant through the provisions of *his* Will and Testament, a document which has been described as 'the Charter of the New World Order which is at once the glory and the promise of this most great Dispensation'. In it he appointed Shoghi Effendi, his eldest grandson and the great-grandson of Bahá'u'lláh, as Guardian of the Faith and required all Bahá'ís to turn to him, promising that '*The mighty stronghold shall remain impregnable and safe through obedience to him who is the guardian of the Cause of God*'.[76]

The Guardian was made sole interpreter of the sacred text, thus protecting the Faith from schism.

Bahá'u'lláh, in a written text, had created the Universal, or Most Great, House of Justice, had invested it with the supreme legislative authority of his world commonwealth and had declared it to be under the guidance of God and in his own protection. Such clear establishment in the sacred text is the warrant to Bahá'ís of the authenticity of its authority and guidance.

'Abdu'l-Bahá, when establishing the Guardianship, made the Guardian permanent head of the Universal House of Justice and provided, on the principle of primogeniture, for a succession of guardians, who would all occupy this position. However, Shoghi Effendi died without issue in November 1957, some five and a half years before the Bahá'í world community was sufficiently developed, according to his plan, to elect the Universal House of Justice. This institution was, as foreseen by him, elected in 1963 and now perpetuates to the Bahá'í world that divine guidance which is the unique feature of Bahá'u'lláh's Covenant.

The effectiveness of that Covenant has already been proved in the short but stirring history of the Bahá'í era. The periods of crisis arising with the successive departures of Bahá'u'lláh and 'Abdu'l-Bahá, were used by the enemies of the Faith for attempts to disperse its followers and make divisions. Many sought leadership and repudiated the Covenant, but none was able to create a following or establish a sect. Today, with the influence of the faith extending to every part of the world, the unity of its followers is unimpaired; rather does it become strengthened with each passing day, with each new effort made for the spread of its teachings.

Spiritual Assemblies

Every local Bahá'í community elects its own ruling body, an institution created by Bahá'u'lláh and called the House of Justice. At the present time these bodies, of which there are several thousand throughout the world, are called Spiritual Assemblies.

The principle and method of election is unique. There are no nominations, no candidates, no parties; to attempt to influence another's vote is an offence which is punishable, and can invalidate an election.

Every member of the community who has attained twenty-one years of age has the vote. The Spiritual Assembly has nine members,* and every adult member of the community is eligible for election. Therefore in a prayerful attitude the community meets and each member casts nine votes, writing down only the names of those people whom he or she feels best fitted to be entrusted with the direction of the community's affairs. When voting, the qualifications borne in mind are, first character, then training, capacity, maturity of experience. Social or financial qualifications do not exist. The nine people polling the largest number of votes constitute the membership of the Spiritual Assembly.

* Bahá'u'lláh's instruction is nine or more; at present nine is adhered to.

This body has full jurisdiction over all the affairs of its community. It is the Trustee, the Servant, the court of appeal, the administrator of all local affairs. It fosters the spiritual and material development of its community. It elects its own officers such as a chairman, secretary, treasurer, etc., and appoints committees to look after the varied activities of community life. It is through its committees that the Spiritual Assemblies can engage for the benefit of the community, that specialized knowledge which it may not—probably will not—have in its own membership.

Members of the Spiritual Assembly have no power or privilege as individuals. It is only as an administrative body, deriving its existence from the Scripture, that it has authority.

The celebration of festivals, and other special occasions, is arranged by the Spiritual Assembly. In providing for these and other meetings for worship, it makes full use of the talent of the whole community. Music, reading of prayers, of passages from the Scripture, talks on spiritual matters, are provided by all members of the community upon request, according to their talent. There is no set form, and ritual is forbidden. Any person may be asked by the Spiritual Assembly to conduct a meeting, or to arrange it in his own way.

The Spiritual Assembly must report to the community once every nineteen days, discuss all matters with it, and receive recommendations which it is bound to consider seriously, but need not adopt unless convinced of their value. Financial and secretarial statements are presented and are open for discussion. There is no secrecy in administration or in relationships with other communities.

In certain geographical areas, generally—though not always—conforming to national boundaries, local communities combine in the election of a National Spiritual Assembly. This secondary House of Justice is specifically instituted by 'Abdu'l-Bahá in his Will and Testament. It is elected on the same non-political principles as the local Spiritual Assembly, and has the same number of members. Each local community elects delegates, either directly to a national convention, or indirectly through area conventions, and these delegates elect the National Spiritual Assembly from the whole body of the national community. The complete absence of candidates, nominations or canvassing ensures that only people of known distinction will be elected.

The National Spiritual Assembly has the direction of all national affairs, and acts as a court of appeal from a local Spiritual Assembly. It unifies the local communities under its jurisdiction and represents the national community in relationship with the Universal House of Justice, and with communities outside its national area.

The Universal House of Justice is elected by the members of the national Houses of Justice. The number of members is not specified; at present there are nine.

This threefold structure, local, national and universal, provides the perfect means for unity without suppression of local autonomy, and for the fullest local development without damage to the world community.

Consultation

The principle by which these administrative bodies work, is that of consultation, a procedure far in advance of the old-fashioned debate.

In debate, an individual or representative of a party enters the Council determined to get his idea put into law. And every political trick, surprise tactics, play upon party loyalties, oratory and other powers of persuasion, are used to accomplish this end.

In Bahá'í Administration there are no political parties or other factions. Problems to be discussed are worked out in a spirit of truth-seeking and prayer. If a unanimous decision cannot be achieved (and this is unusual) the majority vote prevails. But in this case the decision stands as a decision of the Spiritual Assembly, and not as that of a majority over a minority. All members support it.

Such a procedure calls for a high degree of personal discipline and maturity, qualities which are expected from mankind today. The resultant harmony and unity of effort are part of the promise of Bahá'u'lláh.

*   *   *

The 'new covenant', spoken of in ancient scriptures, has been established. On one side of this Covenant is the Most Great Peace and on the other obedience to the appointed successors of Bahá'u'lláh—'Abdu'l-Bahá, the Guardian, and the Universal House of Justice. This august institution has been given full authority to apply the laws and principles of Bahá'u'lláh's Revelation and to supplement those laws whenever necessary. And while it may not change any provisions of the sacred text, it may, as circumstances require and at its own discretion, abrogate its own enactments and apply the Laws of Bahá'u'lláh according to conditions. It is thus both flexible and firmly founded.

This institution will be maintained throughout this Dispensation, and since it prevents the schism which has decimated previous Faiths, religion at last is become the source of unity in the world.

2

In the World Order of Bahá'u'lláh the centre of each community is the House of Worship (called in Persian Mashriqu'l-Adhkár or 'Dawning Place of the praise of God'). From it the spiritual life of the community is diffused. There are no set services, liturgies, creeds or ritual in the purified religion of this day, so the Temple is a place for meditation, prayer, and the reading of the revealed Word. It is to be surrounded by dependent institutions such as a university, school, orphanage, hospice, hospital, research laboratory; these are accessory to the House of Worship and not separate institutions.

In the Bahá'í commonwealth the affairs of each community throughout the world will be administered by the local House of Justice. The work of these bodies will be co-ordinated by the National Houses of Justice, which in their turn will be unified by the Universal House of Justice, the supreme and ultimate authority of the Bahá'í world. Certain universal laws, revealed by Bahá'u'lláh in the *Kitáb-i-Aqdas*—The Most Holy Book—will prevail throughout the world, but local affairs and national affairs will be conducted by the respective local and national bodies. Children in school will learn the universal language and script but they will also learn their native tongue. 'Unity in diversity' will be preserved.

It must be strongly emphasized that this Administrative Order is not in any way separate or distinct in purpose from the spiritual truths which lie enshrined within the revelation of Bahá'u'lláh. Neither can it be regarded as a mere ecclesiastical organization. Rather is it the channel through which the spiritual energy evoked by Bahá'u'lláh, in the hearts of a regenerated race, may find direction and purpose. The new principles proclaimed by Bahá'u'lláh cannot be contained within existing institutions, which have been developed in times of racial, class, religious, and national antagonisms. The universal age requires universal institutions: they have been created by Bahá'u'lláh and 'Abdu'l-Bahá.

Shoghi Effendi, writing of this Administrative Order says: 'It will, as its component parts, its organic institutions, begin to function with efficiency and vigour, assert its claim and demonstrate its capacity to be regarded not only as the nucleus but the very pattern of the New World Order destined to embrace in the fulness of time the whole of mankind.'[77]

'The world's equilibrium hath been upset through the vibrating influence of this most great, this new World Order. Mankind's ordered life hath been revolutionized through the agency of this unique, this wondrous System—the like of which mortal eyes have never witnessed.'*

Man is to find peace and security within its shelter, although the flame of an ordeal more severe and prolonged than any which has chastened humanity, may be necessary to transmute the savage hatreds of this century into active fellowship. But through the pain and chaos of these years, the foundation of world unity has been laid, *'upon an unassailable, an enduring foundation. Storms of human strife are powerless to undermine its basis, nor will men's fanciful theories succeed in damaging its structure.'*†[79]

---

* Bahá'u'lláh.[78]

† For deeper discussion of the political and social theory of the Bahá'í Administrative Order, see the writer's *A Commentary on the Will and Testament of 'Abdu'l-Bahá.* (George Ronald, London.)

CHAPTER IX

THE OUTLOOK

THE new era is little more than a hundred years old. Its infancy has been characterized by two processes, both clearly recognizable, and both increasing in power and momentum as the years have unfolded. One is a process of disintegration, the other of construction. The first has reached its inevitable catastrophic end; the second, struggling and largely inarticulate, presses on to its full development.

The process of disintegration is marked by the fall of monarchies and empires, the breakdown of long established sanctions in the political, social, and religious life of mankind, the increasing clash of economic interests, the overthrow of conventions in both East and West, the undermining of family life and the stability of the marriage bond, the growth of scepticism, self-interest and atheism, and the dulling of the creative instinct by the cinema, radio, and long hours of monotonous work. In the international sphere it is most clearly marked by the failure of nationalism and national economic policies.

The process of construction is associated, indirectly and directly, with the Faith of Bahá'u'lláh. In the increasing spread of those universal principles for which its founders, and at least twenty thousand of their followers, suffered persecution and martyrdom, is seen the indirect effect of their message. Apathy has changed to chaotic activity, and the spirit of world unity, of peace and true religion has penetrated the dead body of the world. Men and women throughout the five continents, unconscious of its source, have inhaled the fragrant breath of the new dawn. Peace movements, moral revivals, world unity societies, a growing liberalism of thought and behaviour are undeniable signs of the new age. Close to the start of the twentieth century the first conference for world peace was held at The Hague, inaugurating a movement which in spite of constant opposition and abysmal failure has grown with each passing year.

'The fierce opposition which greeted the abortive scheme of the Geneva Protocol; the ridicule poured upon the proposal for a United States of Europe which was subsequently advanced, and the failure of the general scheme for the economic union of Europe, may appear as setbacks to the efforts which a handful of foresighted people are earnestly exerting to advance this noble ideal. And yet, are we not justified in deriving fresh encouragement when we observe that the very consideration of such proposals is in itself an evidence of their steady growth in the minds and hearts of men? In the organized attempts that are being made to discredit so exalted a conception are we not witnessing the repetition, on a larger scale, of those stirring struggles and fierce controversies that preceded the birth, and assisted in the reconstruction, of the unified nations of the West?'*

A growing internationalism, the emancipation of women, the spread of education, the movements for a universal language, the great advance in social services and security, the increase in political and religious freedom, are all signs of the spirit of the age. These things, having provoked a passionate and bitter reaction, are on trial today. They must either go on to their fullest expression, or perish as unsubstantial dreams.

This constructive process is directly related to Bahá'u'lláh in the growth of a world-wide community bearing his name and identified with his teaching.

The passing of 'Abdu'l-Bahá in 1921 marked the end of the heroic, or apostolic age of the new dispensation. Protected by the Covenant from schism, the Faith of Bahá'u'lláh entered its formative age, the first period of which was marked by the inspired, dynamic leadership of its beloved Guardian. Gradually developing the potentialities of his little band of 'co-workers', he uncovered to their eager gaze the glorious vision of the Kingdom of God on earth, which it was their destiny to promote. He called them to spiritual discipline, self-sacrifice and heroism, and never ceased to challenge them with greater and greater tasks.

Though small in numbers and resources, without

* Shoghi Effendi, *The Goal of a New World Order*, (1931).[80]

professional missionaries, without the advantages of money and prestige which less dynamic movements enjoy, purely through the untiring efforts of devoted servants, imbued with the love and aided by the spirit of Bahá'u'lláh, the tidings of the new Revelation were spread around the earth and the administrative institutions of the Faith were established in all continents, not only in populated cities but in remote and inhospitable places and in the islands of the sea.

When Shoghi Effendi became Guardian in 1921, the Faith of which he was the head was established in thirty-five countries. When he completed his ministry in 1957 the Faith had spread around the earth and its world-wide community was engaged in a ten-year crusade, designed and launched by him, which was to bring it in 1963—the centenary of Bahá'u'lláh's Declaration of his mission—to a peak of victory and jubilation which was celebrated by nearly seven thousand Bahá'ís from all parts of the world in London's Albert Hall. They heard with awe and gratitude that the Faith was now established in over eleven thousand centres of the earth, that its literature was translated and printed in more than three hundred languages, and above all that the members of fifty-seven National Spiritual Assemblies had just elected, for the first time, the Universal House of Justice, the guarantor of the unity and future development of the Faith.*

* In 1964 the Universal House of Justice launched a nine-year plan, followed by one of five years and that in turn by the present

'How striking, how edifying the contrast between the process of slow and steady consolidation that characterizes the growth of its infant strength and the devastating onrush of the forces of disintegration that are assailing the outworn institutions, both religious and secular, of present-day society!

'The vitality which the organic institutions of this great, this ever-expanding Order so strongly exhibit; the obstacles which the high courage, the undaunted resolution of its administrators have already surmounted; the fire of an unquenchable enthusiasm that glows with undiminished fervour in the hearts of its itinerant teachers; the heights of self-sacrifice which its champion-builders are now attaining; the breadth of vision, the confident hope, the creative joy, the inward peace, the uncompromising integrity, the exemplary discipline, the unyielding unity and solidarity which its stalwart defenders manifest; the degree to which its moving Spirit has shown itself capable of assimilating the diversified elements within its pale, of cleansing them of all forms of prejudice and of fusing them with its own structure—these are evidences of a power which a disillusioned and sadly shaken society can ill afford to ignore.'*

The promised age is no superstitious illusion; it has been gestating during these troubled years and

seven-year plan; the effect of these plans on the expansion of the Faith of Bahá'u'lláh is seen in the current [1981] statistics which record 130 National Spiritual Assemblies and well over 100,000 centres of Bahá'í activity.

* Shoghi Effendi, *The Dispensation of Bahá'u'lláh*.[81]

is now being born in the labour and agony of universal chaos. This is the darkest hour before the dawn, a dawn vibrant with power, clear with certainty and fresh with the breath of a new spirit. The dark night of misery and oppression will soon be ended. The reveillé has been sounded, calling the human race to brotherhood and peace, and service in a more thrilling Cause than any which past ages could offer.

That Cause is the Cause of Unity, of human solidarity, and it demands a remoulding of the attitudes, institutions, and customs which have been developed in the era of a divided humanity.

Let no one misunderstand the significance of Unity. It is the principle of the universe and is opposed to Uniformity. Unity requires a difference in all things; Uniformity requires congruency. Unity is strong, beautiful, flexible; Uniformity is rigid and colourless. Unity is achieved through strong bonds of attraction, co-operation, common interest, and a realization of the relatedness of all people. It preserves national culture, language, and accomplishment; it upholds local tradition and custom, and repudiates excessive centralization; it requires no one to relinquish sane local and national loyalties. It sets the standard of a wider vision, a broader scope, of membership in the human family. It demands the contribution of every nation, every part of the world to the great structure of the temple of mankind. The world is but one country and it will have one language, spoken and understood by every individual of the race, but everybody will speak the language of his own locality as well. Mankind is but one race and the highest loyalty of the new age is loyalty to one's race, but this does not lessen affection for one's native land. The Unity of the world is the linking together of all its component parts in a single body, each giving something of beauty and worth, so that the resultant harmony is the expression of each part skilfully blended into the strength and majesty of the full symphony.

These are days of titanic spiritual struggle. A new world is coming to birth. As the old one passes, in passion and violence, have no regrets. Be thankful and radiant, confident that the shining day of human brotherhood is here.

Hear the Word of Bahá'u'lláh:

'The time fore-ordained unto the peoples and kindreds of the earth is now come. The promises of God, as recorded in the holy Scriptures, have all been fulfilled. Out of Zion hath gone forth the Law of God, and Jerusalem, and the hills and land thereof, are filled with the glory of His Revelation. Happy is the man that pondereth in his heart that which hath been revealed in the Books of God, the Help in Peril, the Self-Subsisting.'[82]

'Soon will the present-day Order be rolled up, and a new one spread out in its stead.'[83]

REFERENCES

ABBREVIATIONS

B.N.E.   *Bahá'u'lláh and the New Era*, Esslemont, J. E.
                Bahá'í Publishing Trust, London, 1952.

B.W.F.   *Bahá'í World Faith*, Selected Writings of Bahá'u'lláh
                and 'Abdu'l-Bahá. Bahá'í Publishing Trust, Wil-
                mette, Illinois, U.S.A., 1943.

Gleanings   *Gleanings From the Writings of Bahá'u'lláh.* Bahá'í
                Publishing Trust, London, 1949.

H.W.P.   *The Hidden Words* (Persian), Bahá'u'lláh. Bahá'í
                Publishing Trust, London, 1944.

Promise   *The Promise of All Ages*, Townshend, George.
                George Ronald, London, 1961.

Promulgation   *The Promulgation of Universal Peace*, 'Abdu'l-Bahá.
                Chicago, 1922.

S.A.Q.   *Some Answered Questions*, 'Abdu'l-Bahá. Bahá'í
                Publishing Trust, London, 1961.

W.O.B.   *The World Order of Bahá'u'lláh*, Shoghi Effendi.
                Bahá'í Publishing Trust, Wilmette, Illinois, U.S.A.,
                1965.

REFERENCES

1. *The Dawnbreakers*, Nabíl's Narrative. Bahá'í Publishing Trust London, 1953, pp. 38-40. The following three pages are based on the account in Nabíl.
2. ibid. p. 44.
3. ibid. pp. 63-5.
4. *Persia and the Persian Question*, Curzon, George N. Longmans, Green and Co., London, 1892, vol. I, p. 501.
5. *Bahá'u'lláh*, Balyuzi, H. M. George Ronald, London, 1968, p. 10.
6. ibid. p. 11.
7. *Epistle to the Son of the Wolf*, Bahá'u'lláh. Bahá'í Publishing Trust, Wilmette, Illinois, U.S.A., 1953, p. 21.
8. ibid.
9. *The Kitáb-i-Íqán*, Bahá'u'lláh. Bahá'í Publishing Trust, London, 1961. p. 160.
10. *The Seven Valleys*, Bahá'u'lláh. Bahá'í Publishing Trust, Wilmette, Illinois, U.S.A., 1957, p. 7.
11. ibid. p. 36.
12. H.W.P. no. 38.
13. ibid. no. 65.
14. *The Proclamation of Bahá'u'lláh* to the kings and leaders of the world. Bahá'í World Centre, Haifa, 1967.
15. *A Traveller's Narrative*, Browne, E. G. Cambridge University Press, 1891, pp. xxxix-xl.
16. *The Chosen Highway*, Lady Blomfield. Bahá'í Publishing Trust, London, 1940, pp. 219-25.
17. cited *The Story of Philosophy*, Durant, Will. Simon and Schuster, New York, 1927, p. 308.
18. *A Study of History*, Toynbee, Arnold J. Oxford University Press, London, 1935, vol. I, pp. 205-71.
19. ibid. p. 173 and footnote 3.
20. Promise, p. 31.
21. S.A.Q. ch. XLII, p. 150.
22. cited W.O.B. p. 106.
23. cited ibid. p. 107.
24. *John* 14:9.
25. cited W.O.B. p. 113
26. cited ibid. p. 113.

27. cited ibid. pp. 113–14.
28. ibid. pp. 112–13.
29. cited ibid. p. 113.
30. cited ibid. p. 117.
31. ibid. p. 115.
32. *Matthew* 24:35.
33. *John* 16 : 12–13.
34. *Gleanings:* section xxxiv.
35. B.W.F. pp. 193–4.
36. cited W.O.B. p. 36.
37. *Why We Behave Like Human Beings*, Dorsey, George A., Harper & Brothers, New York, 1925.
38. W.O.B. pp. 42–3.
39. *The Bible of the World*, ed. by Ballou, Robert O. Kegan Paul, Trench Trubner & Co. Ltd., London, 1940, p. 91.
40. Bahá'u'lláh, cited W.O.B. p. 109.
41. *Tablet to The Hague*, cited B.W.F. p. 286.
42. cited W.O.B. p. 42.
43. W.O.B. p. 42.
44. *Tablets of 'Abdu'l-Bahá*. Bahá'í Publishing Committee, New York, 1930, vol. III, pp. 577–8.
45. B.W.F. p. 288.
46. *Star of the West*. Chicago, 1913, vol. IV, pp. 34–6.
47. Promulgation, p. 166.
48. ibid. pp. 46–7.
49. ibid. p. 57.
50. ibid. pp. 56–7.
51. H.W.P. no. 29.
52. Bahá'u'lláh, cited W.O.B. p. 198.
53. cited W.O.B. pp. 39–40.
54. cited ibid. p. 40.
55. cited ibid. pp. 37–8.
56. 'Abdu'l-Bahá, cited B.W.F. p. 292.
57. W.O.B. pp. 40–1.
58. Shoghi Effendi, W.O.B. p. 202.
59. cited ibid. p. 202.
60. W.O.B. pp. 203–4.
61. cited B.N.E. p. 157.
62. H.W.P. no. 82.
63. ibid. no. 80.
64. Promulgation, p. 233.
65. *Star of the West*, vol. XIII, pp. 227–8.
66. ibid. p. 228.
67. ibid. p. 229.
68. ibid. vol. VII, p. 84.
69. S.A.Q. ch. LXXVIII, pp. 256–7.

70. ibid. p. 258.
71. H.W.P. no. 80.
72. cited B.N.E. p. 156.
73. Promulgation, p. 182.
74. B.W.F. p. 167.
75. *Mark* 12: 17.
76. *The Will and Testament of 'Abdu'l-Bahá.* Bahá'í Publishing Trust, London, 1945, p. 14.
77. W.O.B. p. 144.
78. cited ibid. p. 146.
79. Bahá'u'lláh, cited ibid. p. 109.
80. W.O.B. pp. 44–5.
81. ibid. pp. 154–5.
82. *Gleanings:* section x.
83. cited W.O.B. p. 161.